# Roger Bartlett

Roger Bartlett is a Master Teacher and Examiner with the British Academy of Stage & Screen Combat (BASSC), the UK's leading provider of stage combat training. He has taught at events and workshops throughout Europe and the United States; schools including the Royal Academy of Dramatic Art and Nissan Nativ Acting Studio in Jerusalem; and has been the stage combat teacher at the Birmingham School of Acting since 2003 and City Lit, London, since 2004.

Roger is also an Equity-registered fight director and has worked on many varied productions for venues including Liverpool Everyman, the Bush Theatre, West Yorkshire Playhouse, Theatre Royal Bath, Southwark Playhouse, the Finborough Theatre, the Gala Theatre, Durham, and Warwick Castle – and companies including Paines Plough, Sell A Door and Iris Theatre. He was the Associate Fight Director for the National Theatre's worldwide hit *One Man, Two Guvnors* by Richard Bean.

For film, Roger has worked as part of the stunt team for the Vertigo Films production *Hammer of the Gods*, the popular TV show *Vikings*, and fulfilled a dream when he was able to kill a zombie or two in *Apocalypse*.

Having started out as an actor, working on small-scale and fringe-theatre productions and student films, Roger still regularly acts and directs for the Company of Ten, an amateur theatre company based at the Abbey Theatre, St Albans. He lives in the city with his wife and cat.

www.fights4stage.com

# STAGE COMBAT: UNARMED

## ROGER BARTLETT

NICK HERN BOOKS
London
www.nickhernbooks.co.uk

*Stage Combat: Unarmed*
first published in Great Britain in 2016
by Nick Hern Books Limited,
The Glasshouse, 49a Goldhawk Road, London W12 8QP

Designed and typeset by Nick Hern Books, London
Printed and bound in Great Britain by
Ashford Colour Press, Gosport, Hampshire

A CIP catalogue record for this book
is available from the British Library

ISBN 978 1 84842 470 8

MIX
Paper from
responsible sources
FSC
www.fsc.org
FSC® C011748

*For Tina.*
*My rock.*
*My inspiration.*
*You are the wind beneath my wings.*

# Contents

# Foreword
*Richard Ryan*

There are few books on stage combat and even fewer written by someone who has professionally performed, choreographed and taught the craft. Roger Bartlett is one of those few who does this professionally – he has tested whether what he preaches actually works in practice.

I have known Roger for sixteen years since he first applied to become a Certified Teacher with the British Academy of Stage & Screen Combat, an organisation which is respected, nationally and internationally, as the leading provider of professional-level stage combat training and assessment within the UK. Since that time I have been impressed with his diligence in improving his own technique and knowledge, and his curiosity in learning more and stretching himself. He has gone on to train in the related skills of fencing and martial arts, and become a member of British Equity's Fight Directors Register, a Master Teacher of the BASSC, and a Certified Teacher with the Society of American Fight Directors. I rate Roger's work highly and have engaged him as a part of my stunt team on two television productions – *Hammer of the Gods* and *Vikings* – and he's also assisted me on various theatre shows, including Bristol Old Vic Theatre's highly successful production of *The Three Musketeers*.

Most stage combat teachers, when outlining their course of study to new students, will ask what those students think is the most important element of the craft. More often than not, the response is 'safety', which is a good and correct answer. However, simply to say that 'You must always be safe' is not enough. The essential issue regarding safety is *by what means* do you achieve it? What practical steps do you take, which processes do you follow? The answers to these questions dictate the fundamental philosophy of stage fighting – and these questions are answered in this book.

This book serves as an excellent reference tool. If one wishes to master the art of stage combat, as with any physical discipline, a book will never be able to replace a tutor. However, what Roger offers here comes very close. He has written his book to introduce the main concepts and principles that inform unarmed stage combat as taught commonly by members of the BASSC. What is unique about this book is that in addition to clear and concise explanations, there is a large online resource of videos to back up the written word.

The book outlines a systematic progression of the key technicalities including practical 'how to' exercises and drills that aim to develop the essential skills of partnering, eye contact, Reversal of Energy, balance and centering, and intention. It will be a great addition to anyone's library and a much-needed resource for students, actors and theatre companies alike.

*Richard Ryan is a leading stunt and fight co-ordinator, whose many credits on screen include* Troy, Guy Ritchie's Sherlock Holmes *films,* Solomon Kane, Stardust, The Dark Knight, *which won the 2009 SAG Award for Best Movie Stunt Ensemble, and all five seasons of* Vikings. *His theatre experience includes productions at the National Theatre, the Royal Shakespeare Company, the Donmar Warehouse, and he served as Master at Arms to the Royal Academy of Dramatic Art.*

# Introduction: Playing Safe

This is a book about unarmed stage combat. Or to put it another way, this is a book about how to beat the living daylights out of another human being safely.

I'll repeat that in case you missed it. SAFELY. There is never any excuse to compromise your personal safety and well-being or that of your fellow actor.

A real fight is something that few people actually understand and so there are many people, and many theatre companies, who do not realise the importance of hiring a fight director for their shows. A fight director's job in theatre is to understand fights – how they happen, how they affect people – and to enable the actors to portray that violence as safely as possible.

The history of theatre is littered with stories of actors getting injured. I have a good friend who was working as an actor in a show and she had to be slapped on stage. No one involved in the production knew anything about stage combat and so it was decided that the slap would be real. It went wrong on opening night and ruptured her eardrum. She now only has about 30% hearing in that ear – just from a 'simple slap'. This incident prompted her to get trained properly and she is now one of the top fight masters in America. She does also say, 'the tear has become a wonderful barometer of sorts and I can tell the coming on of a storm or change of weather... no lie.'

This book is designed to give you an understanding of the basic concepts and techniques commonly used in stage fights. It is meant as a guide only. However good a book may be, I would always recommend that you train in a class with a qualified professional. If you have already had some training then you can use this book as a reminder of what you have learned, or to supplement your ongoing training. If you are involved in amateur, student or fringe theatre then this book aims to give you an understanding of practical techniques and how to perform them safely. It should give you a good basic grasp of the practicalities of staging a fight, and hopefully it will help you to recognise when you need to call upon the services of a qualified professional.

The techniques are arranged by concepts, as taught by myself and other members of the British Academy of Stage and Screen Combat (BASSC) – the UK's leading provider of stage combat training. Anyone who teaches with the BASSC or has studied on a course with the BASSC will be familiar with these concepts and techniques.

Above all, I hope you will be inspired to come and learn this beautiful art form for yourself.

## Partnering

Stage combat is an acting skill and requires both combatants, or partners, to work together to tell the story. When you are acting with someone you cannot just say your lines. You must *speak to* another human being. You must *hear* what the other actor has said and respond to it. A good actor is often described as a *giving* actor or a *generous* actor. These qualities are important in stage combat too.

When learning the skills in this book you should always strive to be the best partner you can be. This means being sensitive to the person you are working with, being aware of their needs, supporting and encouraging them.

To be a good partner you should:

- Be patient with yourself and your partner.

- Respect your partner and their work.

- Do your part of the technique as well as you can.

- Check what *you* are doing first to make sure it is correct before trying to correct your partner.

- Be positive in any feedback you give to your partner.

- Ask your partner if there is anything you can do that will help them be more comfortable, confident and secure in their work.

To be a good fight partner you should always pay attention to your fellow actor, watch them closely, give them the right physical and emotional cues to respond to, and work towards making the *whole* fight as good as it can be – not just your part in it. Be a giving and generous actor in your fight scenes as well as in your other scenes.

## Eye Contact

Eye contact is a vital method of communicating with your partner. It is a means of checking that they are ready for what you are about to do and for them to see that you are ready for the next action. It is an essential part of the cueing system used when performing fights. It helps ensure an ongoing connection between you both, and it also helps to communicate your character's thoughts and emotions, not just to your fellow actor but also to the audience.

Have you ever looked at your fellow actor on stage and seen that tell-tale look in their eyes that says, 'Oh help. I've forgotten my next line'? It happens in fights as well. People do sometimes forget what they are meant to be doing. I have heard of one occasion when an actor had to talk their partner through the whole fight move by move because they had forgotten the entire routine.

Eye contact is a hugely important aspect of stage combat. It helps you connect and engage with your fellow actor, it helps you communicate thoughts and intentions. Eye contact needs to be regular and frequent to maintain that good connection and tell an effective story.

Above all else, eye contact is there to help keep you *safe*.

## Dominant Sides

Most of the photographs and the video footage that accompany this book will show the techniques being demonstrated by a right-handed fighter. Consequently, most of the images show the right hand or foot being used.

This is simply because those of us in the pictures are right-handed ourselves. If you are left-handed and want to practise the techniques with your own dominant side, I heartily encourage you to do so. I have tried to keep the written descriptions as neutral as possible so that you can do this. In fact, I always encourage my students to practise these unarmed techniques on both sides, partly because I believe it assists the learning process to work on your non-dominant side, but also because, in a production, you may be called upon to do something with your non-dominant hand or leg.

So by all means, use your dominant side, whichever that is. But do also feel free to practise slowly and carefully with your non-dominant side.

# Using This Book

This book is accompanied by videos of each technique, forty in total, which show me as the attacker in most contexts, with my brilliant colleagues, Enric Ortuño and Yarit Dor, as my unwitting 'victims'. Whenever this symbol appears ▶ visit the companion website – **www.stagecombatbook.com** – and then **VIDEOS**, and enter the password **STAYSAFE** to access the footage.

Please read the descriptions in this book and work through each technique *before* watching the video. You need to understand the principles – especially how to stay safe – before getting up on your feet. Each video shows a technique being performed slowly, so that you can see the mechanics of the action, and the tricks that the audience should not see. You will then see the same technique performed at approximately performance pace from the audience's point of view. In other words, you will see it as the audience should see it.

Follow the stages described in the book with what you are watching in the videos, and try to ensure that your own actions match them as closely as you can. Use the videos to enhance your understanding of the words written here – but please remember that it's in these pages that the specific details and vital safety information is contained.

# Chapter 1:
# Strangling

'An attack which appears to constrict or squeeze the victim's throat to prevent them from breathing.'

Strangles are the first technique we will look at that use *Victim Control*. This is a safety concept whereby the victim is in control of what is happening, thus preventing them from hurting themselves.

*Reversal of Energy* is another safety concept whereby the energy of an attack is directed away from the perceived direction of force, again allowing the victim to remain in control of the technique. In strangles, it can help us establish Victim Control.

To see how these concepts work in practice, let's look at different ways to strangle someone on stage.

Let's start with the version I always teach first because it incorporates both Victim Control, Reversal of Energy and many other ideas that an actor should learn and be familiar with.

## The Reverse-Energy Strangle

A Reverse-Energy Strangle is when we approach from in front of the victim and use both hands to strangle them. To keep this as safe as we can we need to make sure our hands are in the correct position for the attack.

Hold your hands out as if you are holding a bottle in each hand. Now overlap your hands so that the webbing between your thumbs and forefingers are directly on top of each other. It should look like a U-shaped collar that will fit comfortably around your partner's neck. I refer to this as the 'Safety Collar'. I have also heard it called the 'Dove of Peace' and, perhaps less encouragingly, the 'Butterfly of Death'.

This is the shape your hands will form during the attack.

- Get eye contact first of all, to make sure your partner is ready.
- Raise your hands up to throat height as you approach and keep your hands in line with your partner's shoulders to prevent the risk of accidentally poking them in the face with your fingers.

STRANGLING

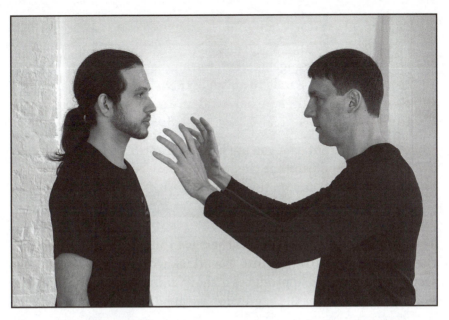

- With relaxed hands and arms, make a sound on the victim's chest by patting both hands against their chest muscles (pectorals). This is called a 'knap'. Avoid striking onto the collar bone – try to find somewhere that is comfortable for the victim. The action should be just like clapping your hands together – nice and relaxed with no force transferred beyond the surface of their chest. Pat onto their chest then bounce the hands off a short distance as soon as you make contact.

The purpose of this knap on the chest is to allow the attacker to take the energy of the strangle into the attack without endangering the victim's throat. It also produces a sharp sound which helps to convince the audience of the aggression we are displaying for them.

- Allow your hands to form the U-shaped safety collar and place this around the victim's throat. The top of your safety collar should rest directly under their jawbone and your fingertips should rest lightly on the side of their neck.

This is where the Reversal of Energy and Victim Control come into play.

> • The victim should now take hold of your arms (just above the wrist – and avoiding grabbing the joint). They are now responsible for pulling the attacker's hands in towards their own throat to keep them in place during the struggle.
>
> • Throughout, the attacker continually attempts to pull their hands away from the victim's throat to make sure they are not putting any pressure on the vulnerable area at the front of the neck.

This is the Reversal of Energy – the energy of the attack is going in exactly the opposite direction to the way it would be going in reality. It also creates tension in the arms of both actors which is exactly what you would expect to see if it was happening for real.

The attacker should pull away with slightly less energy than the victim is pulling in to allow the victim to be in control and to help keep the hands in place during the technique.

These two concepts are the things that keep the victim safe. Because the victim is in control, and because we are using the Reversal of Energy, the victim should just be able to let go and the attacker's hands will then immediately come away from their throat because that's the direction the attacker is pulling them.

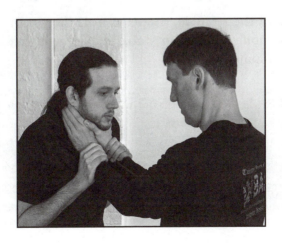

## Dos and Don'ts

- Do talk to each other and check that there is no pressure on the front of the victim's throat.

- Do check that the attacker's arms are not being squeezed unnecessarily hard.

- Don't fall into the stereotyped backwards and forwards shaking action. Not only is this fake but it also puts the victim in danger.

- Don't let the attacker shake the victim from side to side either. Remember this should be Victim Control, so the victim should be in control of all their own movements.

- Do check and make sure you are each in control of your own bodyweight. Don't rely on the other person to hold you up or stop you falling over.

## Dramatising the Strangle

Now that we have the basics of the technique, we need to look at performing it and making it exciting and believable for the audience.

Firstly, we need to create the appropriate physical picture that tells the story clearly and effectively. We call this *Picturisation*, and it is a concept that runs through everything we do in stage combat.

In the story of the strangle, the attacker is the person winning the fight at that moment. So their status should be higher than the victim's at that moment.

- The victim should hunch their shoulders and drop their chin on top of the attacker's hands to help hide any gap that may appear, and to make it look like they are trying to make the target as small as possible.

- The attacker should keep their arms bent during the strangle. This creates a much stronger image for the audience.

- The victim should bend their knees to make themselves look smaller, more vulnerable and weaker than the attacker.

- The attacker should make sure they stay upright and tall so they look like they are dominating their victim.

- The victim can lean away from the attacker slightly as if they are trying to get away. But not too far – they don't want to fall over.

- The attacker should keep a wide, balanced stance to help them look strong and in control.

STRANGLING

Breathing is also important when trying to convince an audience that you are being strangled. Try to avoid the trap of holding your breath. Not only is this unrealistic but it also puts you at risk of passing out.

However, the victim is not going to be able to breathe normally, so how can we alter our breathing pattern to simulate the idea that we are having difficulty getting air into our lungs?

- As the victim, your breath should become more audible as the airway is apparently being constricted.

- Breaths should be taken at irregular intervals.

- Inhalation and exhalation should become irregular and more random. For example, don't always follow your in-breath with an out-breath.

- The breath should be centred a little bit higher than normal to make it seem more desperate and more gaspy. Just be sure that you don't pant or hyperventilate as this can cause you to pass out.

## Intention

Now you have the technique and you have some ideas about how to make it look and sound realistic. There is still one thing missing from a performance point of view and that is *Intention*.

In acting, the terms 'Intention' and 'Objective' can often be used interchangeably.

In stage combat, a character's intention is not the same as their objective. The objective is always 'What does my character want?' Intention, however, is the character's physical and emotional commitment to their objective.

I tend to talk to actors and students about different levels of intention and I encourage them to use a scale of 1-10 where 1 represents 'I want it but I can't really be bothered to try and I don't really care if I succeed or not.' An intention level of 10, however, means 'I want this so much that I will walk through fire, barefoot over broken glass and impale myself on your sword to achieve it – even though it will be the last thing I ever do!'

Different characters and different situations will call for different intention levels. But remember that in reality a strangle is only meant to do one thing – kill. So it is your job as the actor to find an appropriate intention level that gives sufficient energy to the strangle to make it look real to the audience and yet still allow you and your partner to feel safe and confident in performance.

It is up to the actor playing the victim to give us a real sense of the struggle they are going through. The progression of that struggle from shock and fear through to desperation and then weakness as the lack of oxygen takes its toll.

▶ **Video 1: The Reverse-Energy Strangle**

## The One-Handed Strangle

There is no reason why the Reverse-Energy Strangle cannot be performed with just one hand. The basic technique works in exactly the same way.

- Establish eye contact with your partner.
- Raise your hand up to throat height as you approach.
- With a relaxed hand, knap on the victim's chest. This should be performed nearer the centre of their chest because you are only using one hand.
- Slide the hand up to their neck and place it under their jawbone with the soft webbing between thumb and forefinger nice and central. This should be the same as the safety collar in the two-handed strangle described above.

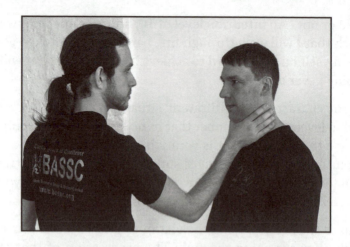

- The victim should then take hold of the attacker's arm with one or two hands and begin to pull in towards their own throat whilst the attacker can now pull away (thus establishing Victim Control by using the Reversal of Energy technique in the same manner as before).

- The victim should still drop their chin down over the attacker's hand and hunch their shoulders as before.

- The victim can alter their breathing as before.

- Both victim and attacker should create the same kind of physical pictures as described above to help tell a clear, strong story.

The story of this version is often less murderous than when strangling with two hands. This one-handed version can often be used to express a certain power or control over the victim, or to threaten and scare them rather than actually to kill them. You need to find a different intention level and a different physical energy to help ensure the story is clear for the audience.

▶ **Video 2: The One-Handed Strangle**

## The Strangle from Behind

The biggest difficulty with the Strangle from Behind is that we cannot get eye contact before we start. Instead, we need to create physical contact by placing our hands onto the victim's shoulders as we approach them, which lets them know that we are about to begin the technique.

- Approach from behind the victim and place your hands onto their shoulders.

- Make sure you are standing slightly to one side so that your head is not directly behind their head. Stand on the side opposite to the arm with which you are going to strangle them.

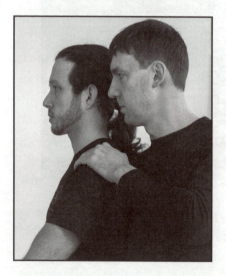

- Holding onto their shoulders, pull the victim back towards you. Their shoulder blade should come to your pectoral muscle and your head should be looking over their shoulder.

- Take your arm out in front of the victim, over their shoulder and reach across their chest to their other shoulder. You are basically laying your arm across their upper chest and holding them close to you. Try to position the arm so that the forearm is lined up centrally below the victim's throat.

- The victim should hunch their shoulders up and hold on to the attacker's arm that is lying across their chest and drop their chin over the arm. This should make it look as if the attacker's forearm is across their throat.

- The attacker should now take hold of their strangling arm with their other hand and pull inwards towards themselves. I suggest bringing the hand up from underneath to hold the strangling arm – it's the same action as a bicep curl, or lifting something by bending the elbow. At the same time, the strangling arm must push away from the victim. This creates the Reversal of Energy and allows the victim to be safe and comfortable inside the frame of the attacker's arms.

## Dramatising the Strangle from Behind

When performing this technique, we must remember to think about the story of what is happening to us and what we are doing to our partner. This will help us create an appropriate physical picture which closely matches the reality we are trying to portray.

In reality, the attacker would be squeezing their forearm against the front of the victim's throat, pulling them backwards and into their chest. In order to relieve the pressure against the front of their throat, the victim would have to move backwards and away from the attacker's forearm – essentially pushing themselves back into the attacker's body.

To make sure the image you present to the audience is as convincing as possible, keep your shoulders and faces up (see left-hand photo) and do not allow yourselves to bend forwards and pull down towards the floor as this only hides both faces from the audience and puts more pressure on the victim's throat (as in right-hand photo).

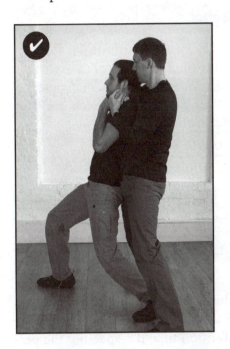 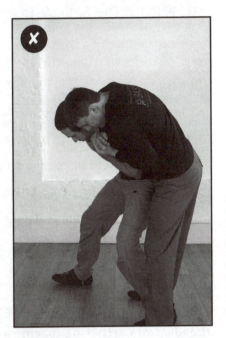

STRANGLING

- The victim should still lower their centre and appear to be vulnerable and weaker than the attacker.

- The victim should still alter their breathing as discussed before to let the audience know their character is struggling to breathe.

- Physical contact between the attacker and the victim should be maintained through the upper body as much as possible.

- Although both actors are sharing physical contact they need to make sure they are in control of their own body weight. Do not rely on your partner to hold you up.

As with other strangles, you must consider the intention level of the attacker, their physical energy and the development of the struggle from the victim. Go through the stages of surprise, anger, fear, desperation. Be creative, and have fun with it!

▶ **Video 3:** The Strangle from Behind

## Summary

- Make sure the victim is in control.
- Make sure there is no pressure on the victim's throat.
- Create the right physical picture.
- Remember to alter your breathing patterns.
- Work out your intention levels.
- Be specific with your story.

These strangling techniques introduce us to the main safety concepts of Victim Control and Reversal of Energy. I also use them to introduce the ideas of partnering (paying attention to and respecting the person you are working with), physicalising a story and intention.

Victim Control will also be used in the techniques described in Chapters 2 and 3 on Pushing, Pulling and Locking.

STRANGLING

# Chapter 2:
# Pulling and Pushing

*Pulling: 'To take hold of a partner and appear to control their movement towards or past you.'*

Pulling someone around on stage is wonderfully deceptive because it is entirely a Victim Control technique, but it is hard to spot because the attacker really does pull the victim.

## The Hair Pull

This technique is great because just about the only difference between the stage version and the real version is how much you close your fist.

- Begin by getting eye contact with your partner.
- As you approach, raise your hand up and bring it towards the victim's head, coming from the side and over the shoulder so you avoid poking them in the eyes with your fingers.

17

- Run your fingers up into their hair as if you are going to grab a handful.

- Curl your fingers over as if closing your fist and rest the flat of the fingernails on the victim's skull. Do *not* actually clench your fist. You should hopefully have a few strands of the victim's hair sticking out between your fingers, but your fist should be relaxed and you should not actually be holding their hair at all.

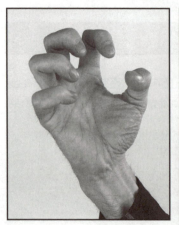

- The victim should now reach up and clamp your hand down onto their head using the hand on the same side of the body as the hand you are attacking with. For example, if the attacker is using their right hand, the victim should use their left hand to secure the attacker's right hand to the head.

- With their other hand, the victim should take a firm grip of your forearm (the same arm that you are grabbing them with).

- The victim is now responsible for keeping the hand secured to their head and not letting it slip off during the pull.

- The attacker's job is to keep the victim safe by looking to where they are about to pull them and checking that it is clear of any hazards such as open trap doors, stray furniture, other actors.

- The attacker should look back over the same shoulder as the arm they are using, then step back away from the victim with the same side leg and turn their hips to pull the victim across their body. This action will allow the large muscles of the back and thighs to be utilised in the pull, which will make it look strong. Just make sure you keep looking to where you are going to pull your victim.

I know what you are about to say. How is this Victim Control if the attacker is actually pulling their partner across the stage? But remember who is actually holding on to who.

It's the *victim* who is holding onto the attacker – so if the victim decides they do not want to be pulled then they can just let go and the attacker's hand should come away from their head safely and without a fistful of hair because they are not really holding on.

You will not always need to pull someone across the stage as violently as this. This technique can just as easily be played as a simple grab, in which case just omit the last step. Remember that this is Victim Control – the attacker should never control the victim's movements, and they should certainly never *push* against the victim's head.

What if the victim does not have enough hair to grab hold of? Try:

## The Ear Pull

The Ear Pull works in exactly the same way as the Hair Pull. The only difference is where the attacker is apparently holding the victim.

- For the Ear Pull, follow the steps as described above for the Hair Pull.

- The attacker's hand should be placed around the victim's ear with the bottom of the palm resting lightly on the cheek and the fingers curling around behind the ear. Do *not* actually grab hold of the ear. The flat of the fingernails should be resting on the hard bit of bone behind the victim's ear.

- The victim should still secure the attacker's hand to their own head and hold on to the attacker's arm as in the Hair Pull. The pull will happen in exactly the same manner.

PULLING AND PUSHING

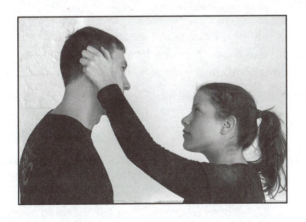

▶ Video 5: The Ear Pull

### Dramatising the Hair or Ear Pulls

Whether you are being grabbed by the hair or by the ear, the chances are it will hurt. A lot. Just about anyone with brothers or sisters will be able to tell you that.

So the actor's job is to express the pain believably. There should be one 'ouch moment' when you are first grabbed, then another 'ouch moment' when you are actually pulled around. The pain should be slightly different for each moment and so may require slightly different vocal sounds to portray that difference. There will certainly be a difference in the level of pain between the two moments.

For me, this is one of the most fun times in class, encouraging my students to explore those moments and really express the pain through their vocal and facial reactions.

## The Drag Along the Floor

We can take the Hair or Ear Pulls one stage further and really get dramatic with them.

- Start with the victim sitting on the floor and the attacker standing next to them facing the opposite way.

- The attacker reaches down and places their hand on top of the victim's head and gently slides down towards their back, fingers pointing downwards.

- Everything happens as for the regular Hair Pull. Close the hand into a fist, but don't really grab their hair. The flat of your fingernails should be resting lightly on the victim's skull.

- The victim will clamp the attacker's hand down onto their head, keeping a strong and secure grip.

- With their other hand, the victim will still grab hold of the attacker's forearm, just above the wrist joint. The victim now has the control over the technique in the same way as before.

- As the attacker walks away, the victim stretches out along the ground and allows themselves to be pulled along. Remember, they can just let go at any moment if they want it to stop.

- Depending on the relative sizes of the performers – and maybe even the strength or secureness of their grip – the victim can actually help by using their hips and feet to push themselves along whilst they valiantly act like they are struggling whilst being dragged.

You may wish to consider the victim's costume and the floor surface before electing to try this. Bare legs, partially exposed torsos and rough wooden stages do not mix very well.

▶ Video 6: The Forwards Drag Along the Floor

23

You can also do this with the attacker facing the same way as the victim. It simply means that the attacker will have to walk backwards and so will need to look back over their shoulder to make sure they don't walk into any trouble.

▶ Video 7: The Backwards Drag Along the Floor

*Pushing: 'To take hold of or touch a partner and appear to control their movement away from you.'*

Pushes are techniques that tend to be overlooked. The overriding opinion is often: 'Well, it's only a push. What harm can it do?'

Frankly, it can bring the whole show to a grinding halt when the person being pushed has their collar bone broken by the impact of the push. Or they fall over and hit their head on the corner of a rostra.

Never underestimate any moment of violence on stage. The actors' safety is paramount and must take precedence over anything else.

Here are two different ways to push someone on stage.

## The Zero-Energy Push

- Establish eye contact with your partner.

- The attacker steps forwards and places their hands onto the victim's chest. Negotiate with your partner exactly where to put your hands.

- The attacker positions themselves with their head lined up with the victim's shoulder to avoid any chance of heads clashing. At this stage the attacker's arms should be almost straight.

- The attacker should now look behind the victim to make sure the space they are going to be pushed into is safe and clear of any obstructions.

- The attacker now steps up with their outside foot (left foot if standing to the left side of the victim), bringing it level with the victim's feet. Allow the arms to bend at the elbow as you step in. Shift your weight forwards, and engage your hips and your core to give the impression of power.

• The victim now takes themselves backwards away from the attacker. The attacker extends their arms again, following after the victim, thus making it look like they have pushed them.

This version of the push ensures that the victim is completely in control of what happens to them. It can look incredibly effective when done well.

 **Video 8: The Zero-Energy Push**

## The Shared-Energy Push

The Shared-Energy Push works in exactly the same way apart from one element. The attacker actually gives energy to the victim to make them move. In other words, the attacker actually pushes the victim. The Victim Control is maintained because both partners *negotiate* with one another during rehearsals to establish a level of energy that the victim is comfortable with and that they can control.

We should be aiming to give enough energy to the victim to allow them to feel as if they have been pushed for real, whilst still being able to control the energy they are given and their resultant movement.

They must not lose control and fall over or crash into anything – unless this is part of the planned action, of course.

With this version, the use of the hips and the core for the attacker becomes more important – especially if the victim is physically bigger than the attacker. To allow the audience to believe that a smaller person is capable of pushing someone larger than them, they must utilise the large muscles in the legs and the back by bending the knees, turning the hips and shifting their body weight through the attack.

 **Video 9: The Shared-Energy Push**

### Summary

- Always look where you are sending the victim to make sure it is safe.
- Use your hips for strength and power.
- The victim must still be in control.
- Vocalise and share the pain with the audience.
- Look after your partner and they will look after you.

These are all still Victim Control techniques. But it is the attacker's responsibility to keep the victim safe by making sure the space they are moving in is clear.

I should also add an important piece of advice here – *'The victim has the final say.'* In other words, if the victim says that what we are doing to them is uncomfortable, then they are right (regardless of what we think). But at the same time if they say everything is OK, then it's OK (regardless of what the demon voice in our own head is telling us!).

I find that these techniques are good for developing partnering and storytelling skills. They also demonstrate how important the hips are when trying to control the movement of another person.

# Chapter 3: Locking

*'An offensive action that manipulates a joint to force it past its normal range of motion – causing pain and controlling the victim's movement. If the manipulation is continued, it can lead to breaking the joint.'*

This section is *not* concerned with how to apply locks for real. We do occasionally explore this in class with qualified instructors under controlled conditions, but this book is about violence for the stage. Therefore I am focusing here on the *appearance* of applying a lock and how two actors can safely tell a convincing story to the audience.

There are many, many different types of lock that can be applied. Here are just a few that could be useful in theatrical situations.

## The Wrist Lock

The Wrist Lock is a good controlling technique, which is simple and very effective. It can be applied from a number of different starting positions, but I am going to assume that the attacker has grabbed the victim by the shirt or jacket.

- Establish eye contact with your partner.

- The attacker then takes hold of the victim's hand, placing their own thumb against the back of the victim's hand and their fingers wrapping around into the palm of the hand.

- The victim now takes control and simply flexes their wrist, bringing the palm of the hand towards their forearm and rotating the hand to form a twisted and painful image.

- As the victim flexes their wrist, the attacker can take a step back away from them.

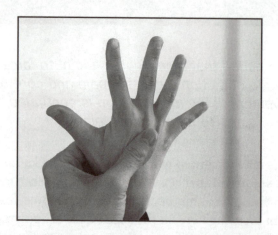

- The victim should also allow their arm to bend slightly at the elbow.

- Make sure only to rotate or flex as far as is comfortable for you. Remember that this is Victim Control so if you hurt yourself it's your own fault!

- The attacker must keep a secure but relaxed grip on the victim's hand and go along with the victim's movement to make it seem like they are the person making it happen.

- If you want to, the attacker can add their other hand to give the impression of extra force and control.

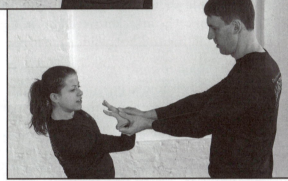

## Dramatising the Wrist Lock

As with everything else, it is essential to *act* the technique. Or more precisely, to act the story of what is happening at that precise moment.

Remember that locks are designed to cause pain, so the victim must show that pain to the audience.

- Be specific about where the pain is.
- Be clear in your own mind about what type of pain it is and how much it hurts.
- Express that pain vocally as well as through your physicality, facial expression and body language.

- Keep the physical picture as large as you can manage – so that the audience get to see what is going on more clearly – by keeping the arm stretched out with some distance between victim and attacker.

- The victim must remember to keep their face open to the audience so they can see the victim's pain and emotions. Don't exclude them by hiding your face or looking down at the floor the whole time. Share it with them.

This technique is about timing and storytelling. Because the victim does all the work, the attacker needs to time their movements with those of the victim and both sides must play their objectives and intention levels.

Chapter 9 describes how to portray pain, and the different things that the actor needs to think about to make the pain seem as real as possible to the audience.

 **Video 10: The Wrist Lock**

## The Arm Lock

The Arm Lock is very similar to the Wrist Lock, but it is actually being applied to the larger joints in the arm – elbow and shoulder – rather than just to the wrist. It makes a bigger impact and can be very dramatic.

- Begin the same way as for the wrist lock with eye contact and the attacker taking hold of the victim's hand, with their thumb to the back of the victim's hand, and their fingers wrapped around into the palm. Use the same side hands – right hand to right hand, or left hand to left hand.

- The attacker places the palm of their other hand on the victim's triceps/upper arm about halfway between the elbow and the shoulder. Keep the hand open and make sure not to apply any actual pressure.

- The victim must again take control and be responsible for their own movement.

- The victim straightens their arm and rotates forwards from the shoulder.

- The victim may also lean forwards from the waist, lower their centre and bend the knees slightly. But they should keep their head and shoulders just above the level of the hips.

- The attacker should step in towards the victim's side and ensure they are facing the same way as the victim, preferably out towards the audience.

- The attacker should stay as upright and as balanced as possible to help create the image of being dominant and in control.

This technique can be a bit of a bug-bear for people who are trained in how to apply locks for real. A friend reminds me that if this technique were applied correctly (for real) then the victim would end up face down on the ground very quickly indeed. I have absolutely no reason to doubt this or dispute it. I do, however, like to think of the theatrical side to things as well as the martial reality, and I find it theatrically more interesting if the victim is able to stay on their feet. Of course, if the situation called for it, then there is no reason why this cannot take the victim all the way to the ground – it's a choice to be made by the actors, their director and the fight director.

The focal point of this lock, and the primary location of the pain, would be in the shoulder joint, so when you are thinking about dramatising this technique, remember to be specific about where the pain is centred, how far it spreads down the arm to the other joints, and what you might be able to do as a victim to lessen the pain.

▶ **Video 11: The Arm Lock**

## The Backhammer (or Half-Nelson)

The Backhammer is another good controlling technique. It can be used in many situations such as a police officer arresting a criminal, subduing an unruly citizen, or a villain getting nasty with the hero. Yet again it is all Victim Control – and the attacker simply goes along for the ride and looks tough!

- Depending on your position on stage it may not be possible to get eye contact with your partner; for example, if you are standing behind them.

- If you cannot get eye contact then simply place one hand on the victim's shoulder as you approach them (in the same way as you did in the Strangle from Behind).

- If you can get eye contact, then do so.

- With the other hand, the attacker then takes hold of the victim's arm just above the wrist joint and prepares the victim by moving the victim's arm slightly away from the side of the body.

LOCKING

- The victim now takes control and moves their own arm up behind their back as far as is comfortable, whilst the attacker holds on.
- At the same time, the attacker must step up close behind the victim and, if they have not already done so, place their free hand onto the victim's shoulder – the opposite one to the arm you are holding.
- The victim now simply needs to arch their back and play the pain of the lock, and the attacker needs to look mean and tough.

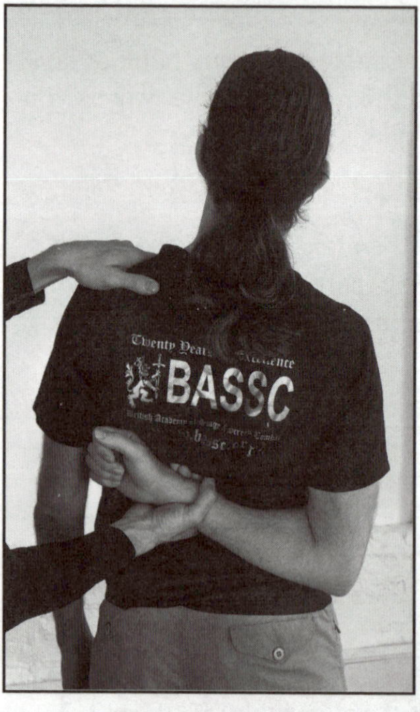


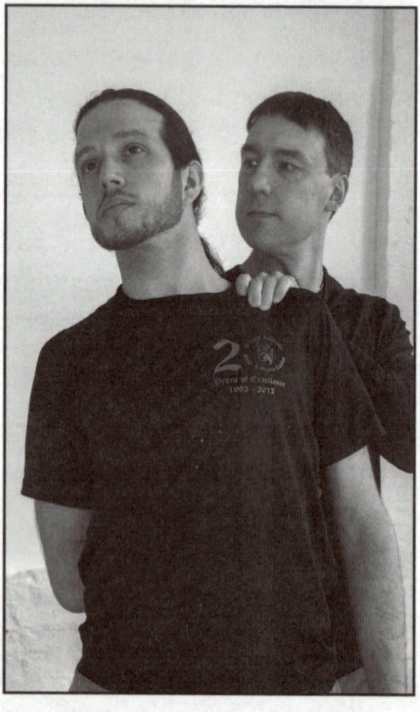

▶ **Video 12: The Backhammer**

## The Full Nelson

The Full Nelson is great fun, but does need a little care. Make sure you are using the Reversal of Energy concept to keep the victim safe and comfortable.

- The attacker must approach the victim from behind.
- The attacker's arms pass through under the victim's arms to the front of their body.
- The attacker's arms then reach up towards the victim's head by bending at the elbow.
- The attacker then places their hands gently onto the back of the victim's head. Do not apply any actual pressure.
- Make sure to place one hand directly on top of the other hand – do not interlock the fingers.

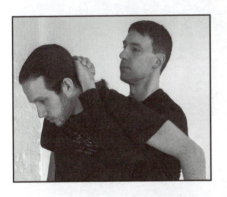 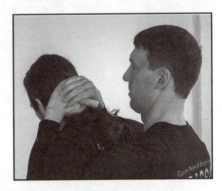

- The attacker can now create the Reversal of Energy by pushing their hands into each other, similar to the method used in the Strangle from Behind.
- The victim then leans their head forwards, taking their chin towards their chest, making it look like the attacker is forcing their head downwards.

- The attacker should stay upright through the body and keep their own head up and back straight to avoid any unnecessary clashes.

- There should be constant body contact between attacker and victim through the chest of the attacker and the back of the victim. This helps to keep things secure and stable, as well as making sure that the attacker's arms can actually reach far enough through to the victim's head.

▶ **Video 13: The Full Nelson**

**Summary**

- Work out exactly where the pain is meant to located.

- The timing between both partners is vital to create the illusion.

- Create a strong, clear picture for the audience.

- Let the audience see that picture.

- Be as specific as you can with what you are doing.

Remember that these techniques still employ either Victim Control or Reversal of Energy. So attacker and victim must work together and time their movements to make it look like the attacker is doing the work. If you are attacking, make sure you engage your body so that you look strong and aggressive, just as you would if you were doing it for real.

Just as with Pulling and the Shared-Energy Push, the victim has the final say. So have fun, stay safe and, above all, listen to what your partner is telling you.

LOCKING

# Chapter 4:
# Falling

*'A way of collapsing to the ground in a controlled manner.'*

The act of falling is often overlooked, but it is quite straightforward and can save you a lot of pain and discomfort. Even experienced people can make mistakes.

I distinctly remember playing Danceny in a production of *Les Liaisons Dangereuses* and falling heavily onto my right hip during the big sword fight at the end. I could not walk properly by the following day and the director had to call us all in early to re-stage many of my scenes because of my injury. So practise as much as you can to reduce the risk of mistakes like this happening to you.

With all the falling techniques, the objective is quite simple. You need to go from standing up straight to flat on the floor without hurting yourself. And you need to be able to do it night after night for however long the run of the show is, as well as numerous times in rehearsals.

The main concepts in use with falling over are *Counterbalance* and *Landing on the Muscle Groups* – or 'using your natural padding' as I often call it.

Counterbalancing allows us to control our centre of gravity for as long as possible and to get as close to the ground as we can before any 'falling' happens.

Because we can't generally use mats on stage we need to use the padding that nature has given us – our major muscle groups. By landing on these soft areas and avoiding your hard boney parts you will reduce the chance of injury.

Everyone is built differently and so these techniques are adaptable. What works well for one person won't necessarily work so well for the next person. Take these concepts and principles and adapt them where needed to make them fit and work for *your* body. Get as low to the ground as *you* can before releasing control and dropping. Find where *your* natural pads are and land on them.

When starting out, feel free to use mats to help soften the landing. Many teachers I know will only teach falls if they have mats available for their students to use. I also know many teachers who don't use mats because ultimately you have to do it on the floor with no mat, so you might as well get used to doing it like that right from the start. It's up to you.

## The Big Step Descent (Backwards Fall)

*'A controlled collapse to the ground executed by taking a big step back to allow the body weight to be balanced for the maximum amount of time before committing to the floor.'*

The Backwards Fall is the first type of fall that I teach to my students. It helps them understand the concepts at work and gives them a level of confidence that they can take forwards to the other falls we learn. Here's how it works.

- Take a big step back (about the length of your inside leg), keeping your feet about hip width apart.
- Reach forwards with your hands, as if grabbing on to something to stop you falling.
- Bend forwards at the waist to counterbalance the step back. This keeps your centre of balance between your feet for as long as possible.

- Start to bend the back knee.

- Keep the front leg straight.

- Your hips should be travelling back on a downward diagonal, aiming to sit on the floor just behind your rear foot. Keep reaching and leaning forwards to maintain control over your centre of balance.

- Sit onto the buttock of your straight leg (i.e. the leg you did *not* step back with).

- Gradually unroll along the floor, rolling on the muscles just to the side of your spine.

- Keep your arms forwards and shoulders rounded to avoid bashing your shoulder blades into the ground.

- Keep your chin tucked in to avoid hitting the back of your head on the floor as you unroll.

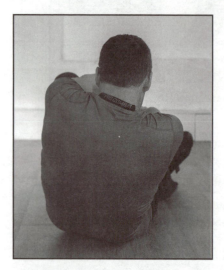

It is always a good idea to breathe out as you go down to the ground. This will help you to stay relaxed and flexible. Holding your breath turns you into a hard, rigid object which will have no suppleness or give in it when it hits the hard, rigid floor.

Try to visualise yourself laying out along the floor, thus distributing your energy rather than dropping onto the ground. I often find it helps to visualise laying out onto my nice, comfortable bed!

 **Video 14: The Big Step Descent**

## The Front Fall

Falling forwards follows the same basic ideas as the Big Step Descent. But now you need to take the big step forwards onto a diagonal so you have somewhere to put your body, and you need to make sure you don't allow your knees to drop onto the floor because that will hurt.

Remember to breathe out as you go down to the ground. It will help to keep you relaxed and flexible.

- Take a big step out onto the front diagonal line in relation to your line of travel.

- Allow the front knee to bend to help you get as close to the ground as you can.

- Lean forwards from your waist and reach onto the opposite front diagonal with the hands.

- Place your hands carefully onto the ground – do not drop onto your hands with all your weight. Keep the hands far enough apart that your body can easily fit between them.

- Pull your hips and stomach forwards and lay down by placing the thigh muscle of your rear leg, the abdominals and then the chest onto the floor.

- Turn your head to one side so that your face does not hit the floor.

- Keep the back leg straight and the front knee up to prevent them hitting the floor.

- Once you are completely on the ground the arms can shoot out to the sides so they do not appear trapped or unnatural.

Use your long step and the big muscles in the thigh to absorb your energy and reduce your rate of travel. The lean forwards will ensure you can place your hands onto the floor rather than dropping heavily onto them. I try to imagine this big step acting as my brake – the length of the step along with the muscles in my thigh will help control and absorb the energy so I can control my landing.

▶ Video 15: The Front Fall

## The Fainting Fall

Fainting is a remarkably effective technique on stage. When performed well it can really produce some gasps from the audience. And, as one director I know puts it, 'Gasps is good.'

- Start with your feet together, standing up nice and straight.
- Bend at the knees, getting as low as you can. Keep the body upright at this stage.
- Start to push the hips out to the side you are going to fall to as you gently turn the body and raise the same side arm up and out of the way.

- Sit onto the buttock just to the side of your feet.
- Extend out on the floor along your side keeping the arm up and reaching out above your head.

- Lay on the side with your arm acting as a cushion between your head and the floor.

This should appear to be an elegant collapse to the floor. It is the archetypal swoon if you like, so breathe out all the way down to stay nice and relaxed.

Use your thighs and your core muscles to control the initial descent until you are sitting on the floor then lay out along your side.

You can go onto your back instead of the side if you prefer. Once your buttock is on the floor you just need to keep the body turn going a little more until you can lay out along your back muscles. Make sure to keep your head tucked in to avoid hitting it on the floor.

 **Video 16: The Fainting Fall**

**Summary**

- Practise slowly to build control.

- Use mats if you wish when starting out.

- Get as close to the ground as you can before falling.

- Land on your muscles.

- Breathe out all the way down to the ground.

FALLING

I often get asked, 'How fast should these falls be in performance?' Well, the only answer I can give is this: The fall must be fast enough for it to look believable within the context of what has caused you to fall over in the first place, but not so fast that you cannot control it.

I would urge you to keep it slow while you are practising and building your confidence. Make sure you understand how to maintain the physical control and how to find the soft muscle groups when you land, before you start speeding up.

# Chapter 5: Slapping

This is the point in the book where we talk about hitting each other. All the techniques in this chapter and the next are non-contact strikes.

*Non-contact: 'Any move or action which does not require any form of contact between the combatants.'*

*Non-contact strike: 'A blow delivered with the illusion of contact, properly masked from the audience, with a well-timed knap.'*

Before we look at various techniques, we need to understand a few things. These will help to not only keep us safe, but also to ensure the story we are telling is as clear and precise as possible.

## Staying Safe

Two things above all else will help keep you safe when performing stage combat and especially non-contact strikes: *Eye Contact* and *Distance*.

Quite simply, if you are too far away to hit someone then you can't hurt them. This is known as working 'out of distance'. Obviously there is a limit to how far away you can be and still make the technique look real, but it is always better to be too far away than to be too close. At least you will be safe.

## The Five Essential Elements

Every non-contact strike needs to have five elements in order for an audience to believe it:

- *The Action*
- *The Reaction*
- *The Knap*
- *The Illusion of Contact*
- *Timing*

The *Action* is the attack itself, which I often break down into three parts:

1. The preparation (showing your partner and the audience what is about to happen).

2. The striking movement (or the attack itself).

3. The after-picture (showing the audience what just happened).

The *Reaction* is the victim's physical movement caused by the action.

The *Knap* is the sound we create to simulate the sound of contact.

The *Illusion of Contact* is how we make the audience believe that contact has actually happened when it hasn't. This is partly about making sure you and your partner are positioned correctly on stage so that you are hiding all the tricks and gaps, but it also involves an idea known as 'crossing the line'.

Imagine an invisible line that travels from the audience's eye to the target and beyond. It is a straight line and it is magic so it can travel through any object that may be in its way without deviating. The striking object (your hand, your fist, a tray, a baseball bat) *must* cross this 'magic line' for the audience to believe that contact has been made with the target.

We should also understand that when we work in the upstage/downstage plane, the audience lacks depth perception. In other words, they cannot tell how far apart two people are (or two objects) unless they have some form of external guide like a nearby table, or unless we show them how far apart we are. So if we perform the action or attack exactly as we would if we really were close enough to do it for real, *and* if we are positioned correctly on stage to hide the gaps, *and* if we cross the line – the audience will believe that we have actually made contact with the target.

*Timing* is critical. We need to time all the elements carefully, so that it looks like the action has caused the victim's physical reaction and the sound.

Now that we have talked about the theory, let's have a look at how we can put these ideas into practice with a few common techniques.

## The Upstage/Downstage Slap

This is a good attack to begin with as it really helps you understand what we have been talking about with the five essential elements of non-contact strikes.

This slap is an attack with the palm of the open hand, generally delivered to the face and it works in a proscenium format where the attacker is standing upstage and the victim downstage with their back to the audience.

First of all, make sure you are at a safe distance by standing far enough away from your partner so that you cannot touch them with a fully extended arm, and establish eye contact to ensure you are both ready.

## The Action

The action is the attacker's movement.

> • Make the preparation for the attack by raising your open hand up next to your face. Extend your other arm and point at your partner to reassure them and yourself that you really are too far away to actually hit them.

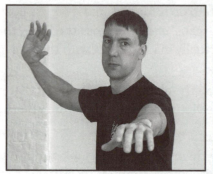 

The preparation is so important in all of our attacks because it helps our partner and the audience see what is about to happen and allows them to follow the story. We talked about picturisation with the strangle, and it's a concept that continues through all of these attacks as well. By making a good, clear preparation at the height you want to attack, you create a clear picture that the audience can see and understand. It helps support the story you are trying to tell.

- Keep your attacking arm bent as you sweep the hand horizontally past your partner's face, with the fingers pointing up towards the ceiling. Try to lead this sweep with the palm of your hand, as if the palm is travelling towards your partner's cheek.

- As your hand passes their face, allow the palm to turn slightly to face them. This helps signal the apparent moment of contact and helps build the illusion that you have just hit them.

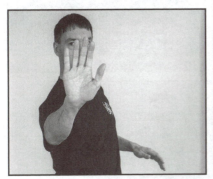

- Continue the sweep of the hand all the way to the other side of your body.

- Finish with the open hand at about the height of your own face, to give a clear after-picture, showing the audience what you have just done. Hold this position for a brief moment – no longer than a heartbeat or two.

- Finally, allow the arm and hand to relax back down to a natural position ready to do whatever is required next.

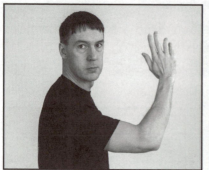

## The Reaction

The reaction is what the victim has to do.

- Make sure you get eye contact to let your partner know you are ready for the attack to begin.

- Watch their hand as it travels towards you and wait for it to pass your face.

- As it passes your face, turn your head in the same direction.

- Try to make sure you are turning your head before any other part of your body begins to move. As this is the part of you that is being hit it must be the part that moves first in your reaction.

- Make sure you turn your head horizontally and try to keep upright through the rest of the body. Don't collapse.

- Once the head has turned as far as it can then feel free to allow the shoulders to start turning as well.

- You can also add a vocal sound to the story – some kind of gasp or sound of sharp pain to help sell the illusion that you have been hit in the face.

## The Clap Knap

There are many ways of creating the knap. The easiest way is for the victim to create the sound simply by clapping their hands together. Strangely enough this is called a Clap Knap.

- Start with your hands in a natural relaxed position by your sides.

- As you see the attacker's hand go past your nose, simply bring the hands together sharply to make a clap. This should happen at the same time as the reaction.

- Keep the arms and hands relaxed and keep the movement small so it remains hidden from the audience.

- You can, if you wish, bring one hand up to the cheek that has apparently been hit in a gesture to soothe the pain of having been slapped, or check for any damage.

▶ **Video 17: The Clap Knap**

## The Illusion of Contact

Creating the illusion of contact is actually quite a simple thing to do, but how you do it may vary from one kind of attack to another. It depends on what position you are in on stage and what theatrical setting you are working in (proscenium format, traverse, in the round). With this particular technique you should be standing in the upstage/downstage position. If you are in the proscenium format then the victim should have their back to the audience so the knap is more easily hidden. This type of slap can also work if you are in traverse.

Remember that in this position the audience lacks depth perception. If you slap *as if* you really are close enough to hit your partner then they will believe you are close enough to hit them. You do not need to actually *be* close.

Remember to make sure your hand crosses the line by travelling from one side of the body right across to the other side. Be aware of where the audience is and also how wide the auditorium is. Make sure you cross the line for everyone!

## Timing

This is what ties everything together. The reaction and the knap must happen when the attacker's hand passes the victim's nose. This will make it look like the action has caused the reaction and the sound. Here is a little extra tip for you – it is always better to react a little bit late rather than too early.

 **Video 18: The Upstage/Downstage Slap**

## The Backhand Slap

The Backhand Slap works in exactly the same way as the Upstage/ Downstage Slap. The most obvious difference is that you use the back of the open hand to make the attack with.

- As with the first slap, make sure you are too far away to make actual contact with your partner.

- Get eye contact to make sure you are both ready.

- The attacker raises their hand up to face height on the opposite side of their body (i.e. left-hand side if attacking with the right hand or vice versa).

- Keep the elbow bent as before and the fingers pointing straight up. The back of the hand should face towards your partner.

- Sweep the hand around past the victim's face, maintaining the slightly bent arm with the fingers pointing up. Make sure you accelerate through the attack to the very end.

- The victim will react as before, by turning their head as they see the attacker's hand pass their nose.

- The victim will make the same clap knap as before at the same time as before.

- The attacker finishes with their hand at face height on the opposite side of the body to where it started. This after-picture is just a momentary hold before you let the hand and arm relax again.

Both of these techniques work well when you are facing your partner in the upstage/downstage position.

▶ **Video 19: The Backhand Slap**

It is often more desirable, though, to have the actors facing across the stage (or in profile to the audience). So how can we safely slap someone in this position?

## The Profile Slap

There are many different ways of performing a slap when you are stood in profile to the audience, and I have seen a number of them over the years. This is how I currently teach my students and actors how to do it. I think it has a natural feel to the movement, it is relatively simple to perform, and it still adheres to our five essential elements for non-contact strikes.

Firstly, we must work out exactly where the line is that our striking object needs to cross so that we can create the illusion of contact.

When you are facing your partner across the stage, your line of vision runs directly from stage left to stage right (or vice versa depending on which side you are standing). The audience's line of vision therefore is exactly perpendicular to your own, and so the 'magic line' runs directly upstage from your partner's face.

This means that in order to cross the line we must be standing close enough actually to hit our partner with a bent arm. Because we are 'in distance' we need to adjust our targeting and the direction that our hand travels in so that we keep our partner safe every time. Shifting the target in this manner is a concept which we call *Displacement of Target*.

I like to imagine a fluffy stuffed parrot sitting on the end of my partner's upstage shoulder. Don't have it too close to their ear, but imagine it right at the end of their shoulder because this fluffy parrot now becomes the target.

- Get eye contact with your partner then shift your focus to look at the imaginary parrot on their upstage shoulder.

- Reach forwards with your upstage hand straight towards the parrot. Your palm should be facing towards you mostly, with the fingers pointing up on a slight angle. This should be a fairly natural position so avoid making it uncomfortable or awkward. Keep the arm slightly bent.

- Your hand should now be hidden from the audience's view by your partner's head. This is your preparation.

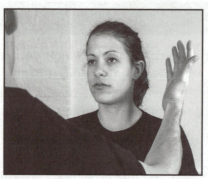 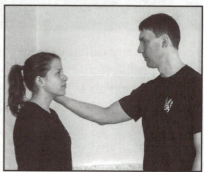

The preparation should be fairly relaxed and not rushed. The emphasis of the attack will be on the next movement.

- Sharply and swiftly pull your hand back towards your downstage shoulder.

- Keep the hand at face height all the way through.

- As the hand comes back past the victim's face you can allow the palm of the hand to turn a little as if rolling around their face. This is a very similar move to the turn in the Upstage/Downstage Slap simulating the moment of contact.

- This is also the moment for the victim to react by turning their head towards the audience whilst making the knap.

- Leave the attacking hand up at face height for a moment to create the after-picture that allows the audience to see what you have just done.

The victim's reaction should be similar to the Upstage/Downstage Slap, but perhaps just a little bit smaller. Try to isolate the reaction in the head as much as you can.

The victim can even use the same clap knap as before. As long as it is kept small and low down it should easily go undetected by the audience. You can, if you wish, make the knap on your upstage thigh with your upstage hand. It will be hidden more from the audience, but the sound it makes is very different and depending on what costume you are wearing this may not actually be a realistic option for you.

The timing of the reaction and the knap are important. When watching your partner begin the attack, you will see their hand disappear from your vision as they reach towards the parrot on your shoulder. When you see their hand reappear in your peripheral vision, that is the time to react and knap. Make sure the reaction is performed at the same pace as the attack.

It can be a little tricky to get the hang of the timing when you first try it out, so I suggest you start slowly. Perform the whole attack slowly and smoothly, and let your partner learn to see the right time to react and knap. As they get more confident with timing it correctly, you can gradually build up the pace of the attack. But be patient.

I believe that this technique is a less violent and aggressive attack than the Upstage/Downstage Slap. It has a smaller range of movement so there is no need to try and make it look or feel as big and strong. Its success lies in its quickness and unexpectedness.

 **Video 20: The Profile Slap**

## Dramatising the Slaps

When you are rehearsing and performing a slap you must think about breath and when your character makes the choice to slap.

The decision to slap someone must happen before you raise your arm. It is the reason you raise your arm. As you raise the arm in the preparation, take a short sharp in-breath through your nose. This should help screw up your face slightly and make it look angry and aggressive. It should also puff up your chest a bit making you feel bigger and more powerful. Let the breath out as you perform the attack to keep you relaxed and free in your movement.

As the victim, you can try making a sound of some sort when you are being hit. What sound you make depends entirely on your character and the situation, but it could be some form of shock noise, or surprise, maybe pain – or maybe the slap stops you making noise (for example, if you have been crying a lot and someone is trying to bring you to your senses and stop you, or if you have been hysterical). Play with a few options before picking the one that works best for that moment.

With all non-contact strikes it is important to rehearse your reaction. Be really specific with which part of the body moves first, how much it moves and at what pace. The reaction should have the same pace and energy as the attack that made your head turn.

Pay attention to the timing of the reaction. Wait to see the attacking hand go past your face before you turn your head. Remember that it's better to be a bit late than too early.

Dramatising the slap is also about having an attitude to what you are doing (or knowing why you are doing it and how you feel about it) and crucially, it is about both characters having an emotional response to what has just happened. Did you enjoy hitting them/being hit? Are you surprised? Do you regret it or do you want to do it again? Do you want to run and hide from them or do you want to hit them back or demand an apology?

Tell the story of what these characters are going through and the audience will follow you. If you just stand and do a technique and have no emotional connection to it they will probably head for the bar.

## Summary

- Be out of distance for upstage/downstage techniques.
- Displace the target if you are in profile to the audience.
- Show the moment when the attacker decides to slap.
- Make sure the head moves first in the reaction.
- Have an emotional response to what happens.

# Chapter 6: Punching

Punches are bigger, stronger attacks than slaps. They are made with a closed fist. The intention is to hit the target with the knuckles or the flat part of the front of the fist. When making your fist, curl the fingers into the palm of your hand and tuck the thumb over them (directly under your palm). Do not put your thumb inside your fingers.

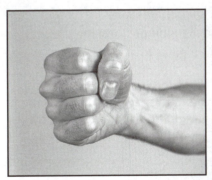 

Because the punch is meant to be bigger and stronger than the slap, we need to engage more of our body in the attack. Use your hips to help you rotate the upper body when delivering the punch to give it the impression of real power. Keep your shoulders relaxed and above your hips to help maintain your balance.

There are so many different types of punch that it would require a whole book to describe them all, so I am limiting the selection here to a few main punches that will serve you well – some that work in the upstage/downstage position and one for when you are in profile to the audience.

Because the attack is now a punch and not a slap, we would expect to hear a slightly different sound when the fist appears to hit the face, so we should make the knap in a different way.

## The Chest Knap

This time, unlike the slap, we will allow the attacker to make the knap. They should use their non-punching hand (the one they point at their partner to check distance in the preparation.)

- Allow the non-punching arm to bend and bring the open hand back towards your chest.

- Keep the hand cupped and relaxed, much like you did in the strangle.

- The hand should strike the opposite side pectoral muscle and pop off the surface of the chest as soon as you make contact.

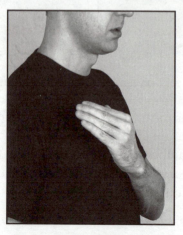

- Keep your elbow tucked in and relaxed by your side to prevent it sticking out and looking awkward and obvious.

- Avoid driving lots of energy directly into your own chest by hitting yourself really hard with a tense, flat hand.

- Make sure you then close the hand into a fist to help hide what you have just done with that hand.

 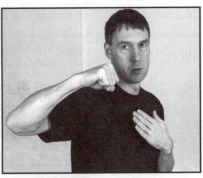

PUNCHING

This is not the only way of performing a chest knap, but it is reliable and relatively simple to execute.

 **Video 21: The Chest Knap**

## The Cross Punch

*'A punch that travels horizontally in a straight line across the target allowing the arm to straighten.'*

The Cross Punch is a terrific and versatile punch. It can suit many different characters and situations.

It works in the upstage/downstage plane, but you can have the attacker or the victim facing the audience – it's up to you. Either way, the attacker's own body or that of the victim will help hide the knap from the audience's view.

- Be far enough away from your partner so you cannot reach them and then establish eye contact to make sure that they are ready.

- Raise your punching hand, bringing the fist up next to your head with the arm bent and the fist horizontal (with the back of your fist facing up to the ceiling).

- As you raise your fist, take a step out with the same side foot and turn your hips to face that way.

- Raise your non-punching hand in front of you and point it towards your partner (this is your distance check).

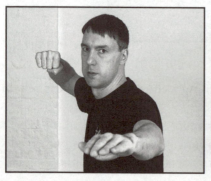 

- To deliver the punch, begin to rotate your hips to face the other side. As they turn you should straighten your arm and extend it fully so that the fist crosses the line of the target.

- As the fist crosses the line make the chest knap as described before.

- The level of the target is the eyes/bridge of nose band across the centre of their head – the Zorro mask if you like. It is important that your fist travels past the victim's head at this level so that everyone in the audience believes you have hit them in the head.

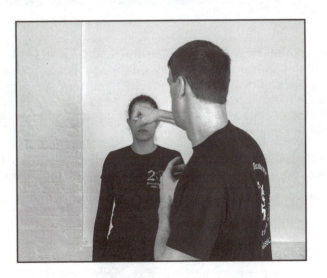

- The victim should react as the fist passes their nose. Turn the head sharply in the same direction the fist is travelling in, then allow the shoulders and maybe even the hips to follow. Perhaps even allow yourself a little stagger step.

- The reaction should be bigger than for the slap because the punch is meant to be a bigger, stronger attack. Just make sure you lead the movement with the head turn because that is the part of you being hit and therefore it would be the first part to turn.

- Once the attacker's fist has crossed the line, continue to straighten the arm until it is fully extended towards the opposite side of the body from where it began.

- Continue to rotate through the hips as much as you can to keep the illusion of power in the punch.

- Allow the fist and arm to finish straight and at head height, creating the after-picture for a moment before allowing the arm to relax down.

▶ Video 22: The Cross Punch

## The Jab Punch

*'A straight punch delivered with a short, sharp in-out action from in front of the victim where the fist travels in a straight line towards the target.'*

Many styles of fighting use the Jab Punch, from boxing to karate. The fighting styles that I have encountered use the front or leading hand to execute the Jab Punch. This allows the dominant rear hand to be used for the bigger punches. On stage, however, we want to use the rear hand to perform the jab so that it stays a little bit safer and becomes more visible for the audience.

The Jab Punch is not the type of punch that will knock someone down to the ground. Instead, think of it more as a softening-up blow, or a distraction move – something that sets up the big knock-down punch (the Cross Punch, for example).

This punch also works when we are stood in the upstage/downstage position, but instead of *crossing* the line to create the illusion of contact, this punch travels *onto* the line. The victim needs to be facing the audience and the attacker should stand facing upstage looking at the victim.

As the attacker, you should stand slightly off-set from the victim. Your punching side shoulder should be aligned with the victim's vertical centre-line. Take a wide, balanced stance with your foot on the punching side slightly further back than your other foot.

The target is about halfway towards the victim's face, level with the bridge of their nose. In other words, the target is the 'magic line' that runs from the victim's nose to the audience (about halfway between them and you). I usually imagine they have a long, rubber Pinocchio nose and I am punching the end of it.

So now you know where to stand and where to aim the punch, let's find out how to do it.

- Establish eye contact with your partner.
- Prepare the punch by lifting the fist up next to your head and turning the hips, pulling the rear hip backwards, away from your partner.

- Now push the same hip forwards again, driving your raised fist in a straight line towards the target. Allow the punching arm to extend, but do not fully straighten it.

- At the moment your fist lines up with the target you should bounce it away from them, as if the fist has bounced back off the end of their rubber Pinocchio nose! Make sure you bounce it back along the same straight line that it travelled forwards on. The fist should be horizontal at this moment with the back of the hand facing upwards.

- At the same instant you need to make a chest knap with your non-punching hand. Keep the hand slightly cupped and knap on the opposite side pectoral muscle and pop off the surface of the chest as soon as you make contact. Then close the hand into a fist again.

As the victim, this is the moment you need to react – when the attacker's fist lines up with the target and they make the knap.

The reaction needs to take your head straight backwards because the punch should be travelling in a straight line towards you. But please do not just throw your head back as this can cause serious pain and discomfort in the neck – it can even lead to whiplash. You want to keep the back of your neck as long as possible to avoid crunching the cervical vertebrae (the vertebrae immediately below the skull) and causing injury.

- Keep your head upright as you pull it straight back and bring the chin in towards the neck.

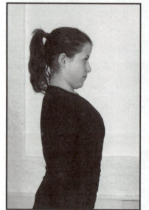
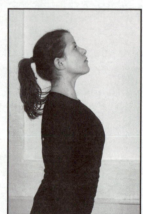

- Then reach up and back from the crown of your head trying to keep the back of your neck extended.

- Take a small step back as if you are staggering slightly as you release and allow your head to settle forwards again by simply allowing the chin to return to its normal position.

- You can also hunch your shoulders slightly at the moment you start to raise the head. This will create a small roll of muscle at the base of the neck which can act as a slight cushion. Make sure you relax the shoulders again as you settle the head.

It should almost feel like a crisp and sudden nod as you pull your chin in to your neck which leads immediately into a raising of the head up and back before then settling and returning to its normal position.

The reaction should be quite quick and small so do not overdo it. Remember that the punch is not a huge 'knock 'em down' punch. So react and return to where you can get eye contact again ready for whatever is going to happen next.

This reaction is a little bit tricky and I will not be surprised if you are having difficulty understanding how it should look just by reading this description. I would strongly suggest that you have a look at the video footage to see it in action. Study it well and practise because a good reaction, well played and well timed, will really help convince the audience that you have been hit.

 **Video 23: The Jab Punch**

## The Profile Punch

The Profile Punch uses similar ideas to the Profile Slap. We must be close enough to our partner so that our fist can reach past their head and we use the same concept of Displacement of Target to help keep us safe. Our positioning relative to our partner is important, so let's have a look at this first.

- Stand close enough to your partner so that with a bent arm you can reach past their head over their shoulder and still maintain a slightly bent arm.

- You should be in profile to the audience again, so facing each other stage left to stage right.

- The attacker should stand slightly further upstage than the victim. Just enough so their vertical centre line is aligned with the victim's upstage shoulder. You can increase this a little if you wish and align the attacker's downstage shoulder with the victim's upstage shoulder.

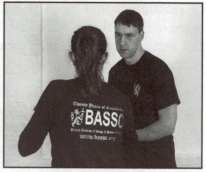

Now let's have a look at how to make this punch work. Don't forget the five elements of non-contact strikes (see page 52) and especially the need to cross the line and create the illusion of contact.

- Establish eye contact with your partner to let them know you are ready and make sure that they are ready as well.

- The attacker should now look to the target, which is the imaginary stuffed parrot stood on the end of the victim's upstage shoulder.

- As you shift your focus to the parrot, prepare the punch by lifting the fist up next to your own head. You should be punching with your downstage arm.

- Allow the hips to engage by turning them towards the audience a little. Keep your knees slightly bent for balance and strength.

- I would encourage you to keep your fist vertical for this punch, with your little finger side nearest the floor, palm facing towards you.

- Keep the elbow of the punching arm down next to your body and pointing behind you.

- The attacker now turns their hips towards the victim and straightens their punching arm.

- Make sure the fist travels in a completely straight line towards the parrot on the victim's upstage shoulder.

- Accelerate right through to the end of the action, as if you are trying to knock the parrot backwards off your victim's shoulder.

- As the fist passes over their shoulder and 'hits' the parrot, you should make a knap. You could use the chest knap, or use the thigh knap described below.

- The victim should look at the punching fist when it is raised up in the preparation.

- As the fist goes past their face and disappears from view, the victim should react by turning their head to look over their upstage shoulder. It is important to wait until you see it go past you before you react, otherwise you could be turning your face into the path of the fist as it travels towards you. Allowing the fist to go past your head before you react allows it to cross the magic line and create the required illusion.

- The attacker should then allow their arm to relax and return to a natural position, or get ready to move on and do whatever is required next in the fight sequence.

▶ **Video 24: The Profile Punch**

## The Thigh Knap

The Thigh Knap is another way to make the sound of contact in a strike. It can be used as an alternative to a Chest Knap when punching, or even instead of a Clap Knap when slapping (I do not think the sound is quite right for this, but if there is no way of clapping then we have to do what we can).

- Use the upstage hand to knap on the outside of the upstage thigh so that it can be kept hidden from the audience.

- Keep the hand slightly cupped and relaxed.

- Try to keep the movement small and subtle.

- Strike firmly against the thigh and immediately withdraw the hand, just as you did with the Chest Knap.

- You may wish to incorporate the knap into a natural movement of the arm, depending on where the arm starts and what your body naturally wants to do.

PUNCHING

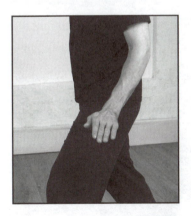 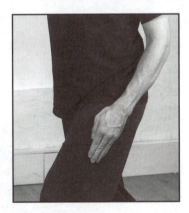

▶ **Video 25: The Thigh Knap**

## The Stomach Punch

Not every punch in a fight will be delivered to the head or the face, so for variety's sake, here's how to do a non-contact punch to the stomach.

It works in exactly the same way as the Jab Punch described above. Start by standing slightly off-line with your punching-side shoulder lined up with the victim's vertical centre line, just out of distance and then punch *to* the magic line that extends out from their stomach.

To help hide the knap and to let the audience see the apparent moment of contact, I suggest that the victim faces the audience, and the attacker has their back to the audience (just like in the Jab Punch).

- Get eye contact then look to the target (the victim's stomach).
- Prepare the punch by pulling the hip back and holding the fist at stomach height. Keep the fist vertical as you do with the Profile Punch.

- Engage your hips by driving the punching-side hip forwards to give the illusion of power in the punch, then extend the arm slightly allowing the fist to travel towards the target.

- As your fist meets the magic line and before it reaches your victim's stomach, bounce it back away from them slightly.

- As you bounce the fist away you should make a knap. You could use the Thigh Knap fairly easily here, but I suggest you do the knap on the front of your thigh this time to keep it hidden.

The victim needs to react at the supposed moment of contact, which is when the attacker makes the knap and bounces their fist away from the target.

- Pull the stomach in quickly and allow your lower spine to curve and push out behind you slightly.

- Pull your shoulders up and forwards to emphasise the arch in your back.

- Keep your head and shoulders above the level of your hips.

- Keep your face up and open to the audience so they can see your facial reactions.

- Make a loud vocal sound as if the air has been forced out of your body and your lungs. This will augment the knap made by the attacker and help convince the audience that you have really been hit.

Just as an extra layer of safety, when you react I would suggest you take your head into the empty space to the side of your partner. In other words, react on a very slight diagonal away from their punching arm and shoulder. This will hopefully help you avoid any unnecessary clashes.

▶ **Video 26: The Stomach Punch**

## Dramatising the Punches

Selling a punch on stage involves the same kind of process as selling a slap. It is important to keep your shoulders relaxed throughout the punch so you can move quickly and effectively – but both kinds of attack rely heavily on the victim to produce a convincing reaction. Without the reaction, the attack is nothing. So do make sure you practise and refine your physical reactions.

As we saw with the slap, the audience really want to see a story and the changing relationship between the two characters who are fighting. That's what they pay their money to see. So make sure you know *why* you are hitting the other person. Make a choice about how you feel about hitting them/being hit. What are the consequences of your actions?

Make sure your characters' intention levels match the choices you have made above. Energise your body and deliver the attack at a pace which will let the audience see clearly just how committed your character is to that attack or that moment of the story. Feel free to experiment with different intention levels and different energy levels until you find the one that best tells the right story.

## Summary

- Be out of distance or displace the target.
- Cross the line with the attack.
- Use your hips and your centre to drive the attacks.
- Great attacks are nothing without great reactions.
- Work out your emotional response to what happens.
- It is always better to react a little bit late than too early.

PUNCHING

Remember to make sure you are in the correct position on stage for the technique you are performing. There is nothing worse than seeing the Cross Punch or an Upstage/Downstage Slap performed by two actors standing in profile across the stage. It's horrible and unnecessary.

Now as you may be aware, not every punch actually reaches its intended target, so that is what we will look at next.

# Chapter 7: Blocking

It would be a short and uninteresting fight if every punch or slap made contact with its target. The reality of what happens when you get hit in the head (the damage, the effect on the brain) makes it somewhat unbelievable. So here are a few ways to stop that big punch in its tracks, or avoid it all together.

## The Cueing System

Attacks that are meant to be avoided or blocked follow a specific sequence of events. Basically, the intended victim must start to make their avoidance before the punch is released in order to remain safe. The cueing system works like this:

- Make eye contact with your partner.
- The attacker then looks at the target as they prepare the attack, thus giving the victim a nice, clear cue.
- The victim begins to make their avoidance.
- The attacker can then perform the attack safely.
- If a block is required from the victim then it is the last thing to happen.

This system is sometimes referred to as *Cue – Reaction – Action* or *Red Light/Green Light*. If the victim does not make their avoidance then the traffic light is *red* for the attacker. The attacker *must* wait for the *green* light which is given by the victim making their avoidance.

Let's have a look at this in action.

## The Roundhouse Punch

*'A punch aimed at the head with a straight arm swinging around in a circular manner which is designed to be avoided by ducking.'*

The Roundhouse Punch is a really big, wide punch. It is generally considered to be a very untrained style of punch. In other words, someone who has not had formal training in how to throw one might throw a punch like this.

It is sometimes referred to as a 'Haymaker' and is a big, wild swing of the arm. It can also be used by comic or drunk characters to great effect.

Because the punch is going to be avoided, there is no illusion of contact to worry about, and certainly no need to make a knap. So you can position yourself pretty much anywhere on stage for this to work, depending on what is going to happen immediately afterwards of course. Just be aware that if you are in profile to the audience it is possible to be too far out of distance and make it difficult for the audience to believe.

## The Preparation or Cue

- Stand just out of distance so the attacker can't quite reach their victim with a straight arm.

- Establish eye contact.

- The attacker should then shift their focus to look at the victim's hairline.

- As you look to the hairline, step out to the side as you did for the Cross Punch. Don't forget to turn the hips out as well.

- Raise the punching arm up, so the fist is at head height and the arm is out to the side, almost straight. This is the victim's cue, so it needs to be clear.

- You can have the fist vertical or horizontal, it's up to you.

- You can also include the distance check with the non-punching hand.

## The Avoidance (or Duck)

A duck is when we avoid an attack by bending the knees and allowing the attack to pass overhead. The timing of the avoidance is crucial. Too early and your character appears to be psychic; too late and the attacker has to wait for you and this just makes everything look fake.

- When the victim sees their cue (the preparation), they should duck by bending at the knees and lowering their head straight down.
- Keep the back straight as much as you can.
- Keep your focus forwards looking at the attacker's hips/centre.
- By looking at the attacker's hips you will be able to see when the attack has finished and know when it is safe to stand up again.

To make it smooth and flow together, the victim needs to start making the avoidance when they see the attacker's arm about two-thirds of the way up in the preparation. This way, when the attacker's arm is in position and they are ready to release the punch, they can see that the victim is already avoiding so they know it's safe to release the punch. This also means that the attacker is not seen to be waiting for the victim to get out of the way, thus making everything much more believable.

Only when you see the victim starting to duck out of the way should the attacker release their punch. If the victim does not duck, don't punch!

- Once the victim starts to duck the attacker can start to punch.
- Keep your focus up high where the victim's head was before they ducked.
- Rotate the hips and pull the fist along behind as you swing the arm through in a circular movement to the opposite side of the body.
- The punch should travel horizontally.
- Keep your knees slightly bent to help maintain your balance.
- Don't forget to show the audience that momentary after-picture before you allow the arm to relax.

This punch should be an open, free swing of the arm, with the fist being pulled along behind the rotating hips and shoulders. It feels like you get ready to throw the punch, then someone grabs hold of your arm as you are about to punch, so your hips and body start to turn but the fist/arm do not move. And then suddenly the arm is released and the fist hurtles around to the other side of your body. This also helps get that all-important acceleration through the attack, thus making it look like you tried to knock the victim's head off!

▶ **Video 27**: The Roundhouse Punch with Duck

## The Bob 'n' Weave Avoidance

The duck described above is a very effective way of avoiding the Roundhouse Punch. But what if you need something a bit more stylish? What if your character is a trained fighter or at least someone with experience? Then you might want a slightly different style of avoidance. Here's how the victim can do the Bob 'n' Weave on stage.

- When you see the preparation, lean your head away from the punch and shift your weight onto that leg. So if the attacker is punching with their right hand, lean to your right-hand side and put your weight onto your right leg. If they are punching with their left hand, then go towards your left-hand side.

BLOCKING

- Whichever leg you have transferred your weight onto, bend that knee to lower your head far enough to take it below the level of the punch. I would suggest you take it below shoulder height at least.

- Lift the foot that has no weight on it and step to that side. As you place that foot down again then shift your weight all the way onto that foot, keeping your knees bent and your head low, so you've shifted your weight from one side to the other.

- Complete the step by bringing the other foot over and standing up again.

Imagine that there is a rope stretched out at shoulder height on one side of you. The Bob 'n' Weave should be like side-stepping under the rope and coming up again on the other side. You should remain facing forwards to your attacker the whole time.

▶ **Video 28: The Roundhouse Punch with Bob 'n' Weave**

As you perform this avoidance, you should remember that it is something that a trained fighter would do. So you should always try to maintain a good balance with your feet apart. Keep your shoulders and your head above the level of your hips and keep looking towards your partner's centre so you can see when the punch has finished. Your hands should also be held in a fighting position somewhere in front of your body.

## The Parrot Punch

*'A punch which travels in a straight line over your partner's shoulder. This punch is designed to be blocked.'*

The Parrot Punch is a very useful attack to know as it can be used with a number of different types of block, some of which are described below. But for now let's discover how the attack works.

There are two fairly important concepts at work here. The first one we have already mentioned – Displacement of Target. This means that the attacker changes where the target is, in order to keep the victim safe. In this punch, the target shifts from the victim's face to the stuffed parrot sitting on the end of their shoulder (just as we did with the Profile Punch). The main difference is that this punch is not meant to look like it hits the victim, so we do not *have* to aim at the upstage parrot. You can, but you do not have to.

With the Parrot Punch, I like to start much further away from my partner. Far enough away so that I have to step forwards to reach them with my punch. This will help make the action look much bigger and stronger for the audience, and it will help you commit to the action whilst still giving you a great sense of safety and freedom.

- Get eye contact with your partner.

- The attacker should then shift their focus to look at the imaginary parrot on the victim's shoulder.

- Prepare the punch by raising your fist up next to your face, turning the hips and taking a slight step back with the foot on the same side as the hand you are punching with.

- When the victim sees the fist about two-thirds of the way up, they can start to make their avoidance – for now let us make this a simple step backwards away from the attacker.

- Once the attacker's fist is in position and the attacker can see that the victim is making their avoidance, then they can start to punch by turning their hips and extending their punching arm straight forwards towards the parrot.

- The punch should travel in a straight line.

- Once the fist is moving forwards towards the parrot, the attacker can step forwards with the leg on the same side (so if punching with the right hand, step with the right foot).

- The foot should land at the same time as the arm reaches its fullest extension.

- The punching fist should be presented in a vertical position, as if the attacker is holding a bunch of flowers. This will present the soft, flat part of the forearm for the victim to block against and avoid the boney edges of the forearm.

- The attacker's fist *must* finish at least level with where the victim's parrot was at the start of the attack, otherwise no one will believe that the punch would have hit the victim if they had not moved out of the way.

The Parrot Punch described here can be aimed at either side of the body. So it could travel straight towards the parrot on the same side of the victim's body, or it can cross the centre line and travel towards the parrot on the opposite shoulder. You simply need to decide beforehand and make sure you both know what is happening.

Similarly, the block can be made with either hand. If you use the hand on the same side as the attack is aimed at, then we call it a Same-Side Block. If you use the hand on the opposite side to where the attack is going then, rather unsurprisingly, it is called an Opposite-Side Block.

The other concept involved now is *Soft on Soft*. This means that we use the soft muscle groups of the arm or hand making the block to connect with the soft muscle groups of the attacking arm when we block the punch. This is really important when you have to do the fight over and over again during rehearsals and in performance. It helps make sure that you do not get hurt, bruise your arms or even break the bones in your forearm.

The most important thing to remember when blocking an attack is *move*! Get out of the way. Don't just stand there and hope your block will be successful, but actually remove the target from the attack. Then if the block does not work for some reason, you still won't get hit in the head!

All of the blocks described below are used against the same Parrot Punch you have just learned.

## The Same-Side Block

If the punch is aimed at the parrot on your left shoulder, then using your left hand to block the punch is known as a Same-Side Block. If the punch is aimed at your right hand shoulder then you would use your right hand to perform a Same-Side Block.

Keep in mind the principle of Soft on Soft. The attacking fist should be vertical so either the inside or the outside of the forearm will be presented (depending on which side the punch is aimed at). So when blocking you should use either the outside of your own forearm, or the palm of your hand or even the back of the hand. Avoid using the edges of the hand or arm because this is where the bones are and this is where you can hurt yourself or your partner.

You should also keep the fingers and thumb together. If your thumbs are sticking out horizontally from the rest of your hands (like a capital H) and you mistime the block, you can get seriously hurt. So keep them tucked in.

There is an old saying in stage combat to help you remember this: 'Hospital. No Hospital!'

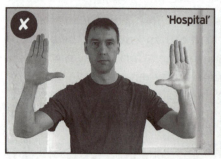 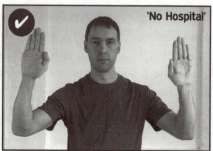

Before you can block the punch you need to decide whether to block with the hand or the back of the forearm. It does not matter which you choose, but each one can say something slightly different about your character and how experienced they are or what training they have had.

Below is a description of how to make the block. Remember that the block happens at the *end* of a sequence. Start with eye contact; the attacker makes the preparation and gives a cue to the victim. Then...

- When you see the attacker's fist about two-thirds of the way up in its preparation, begin to make your avoidance. This simply needs to be away from where the punch is aimed. It can go to the side or straight back or even on a diagonal, just make sure you take your head away from where the punch is going. (So if the punch is aimed at the parrot on your left shoulder, move back or slightly to your right.)

- As the attacker steps forwards with the punch you can begin to raise the hand you are going to block with.

- As the punch reaches its end and the attacker's arm is fully extended, simply place the part of your arm that you are blocking with gently against the attacker's forearm. Remember to keep the thumb tucked in ('No Hospital').

- Your block should stay close to you and your arm should be bent at the elbow. Make sure it finishes in line with your parrot (level with your shoulder). Your block should simply meet the attacking arm and should not push it or beat against it in any way. There should be no sense of impact in the block.

- As soon as the punch has been blocked, the attacker should remove it by allowing the arm to relax and return to a central position ready for whatever is going to happen next.

- Keep your block in position until the attacker has removed their arm.

The following photos show a Parrot Punch aimed at the same-side parrot with the victim performing a Same-Side Block using the back of their hand and the palm of the hand.

The next two photos show the victim using a Same-Side Block against a Parrot Punch aimed at the opposite-side parrot. The first block is with the back of the hand, the second block is with the palm of the hand.

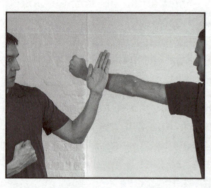

Stage combat is about staying safe and being able to repeat the fight every night. So it should be a 'No Pain' exercise. If you find that the block is causing you pain then something is not working correctly. Check to make sure the attacker is punching with a vertical fist and presenting the soft muscles of the forearm. Check to make sure the victim is also using the soft parts of their arm to block with. Check that the block is not travelling through the attacking arm and 'hitting' it, but that the block is simply placed against the soft muscles of the attacker's forearm.

▶ **Video 29: The Parrot Punch with Same-Side Block**

▶ **Video 30: The Cross Parrot Punch with Same-Side Block**

## The Opposite-Side Block

The Opposite-Side Block works in the same way as the Same-Side Block, but as the name implies, to make the block you simply use the hand on the opposite side of the body from where the attack is going.

You must follow the same sequence of events, and you must still adhere to the Soft on Soft concept. Because you will be using the opposite-side hand though, you should make the block using the palm of the hand. Remember to keep that thumb tucked in next to the fingers ('No Hospital').

As the victim, you will hopefully find that your body naturally wants to turn a little as you bring the hand across you to make the block. Let this happen. It will make the block easier and more comfortable for you, not to mention that it will help you look like a better fighter! Partly due to this slight body turn, the hand will travel in a slightly backwards direction and will 'brush' along the attacker's forearm from near the elbow towards the fist. In effect you are guiding the attacker's fist back past your shoulder rather than deflecting it to the side.

Again you should remember that the block happens at the *end* of a sequence. Start with eye contact; the attacker makes the preparation and gives a cue to the victim. Then...

- Begin to make your avoidance as before (when the attacker's fist is about two-thirds of the way up). This can simply be a walking step backwards, moving the foot on the same side of your body that the attack is going to (i.e. the right foot if the punch is aimed at your right shoulder).

- As the attacker begins to extend their arm and step towards you, and whilst you are still stepping back, you should start to raise your blocking hand (making sure the thumb is tucked in safely).

- As the punch reaches its end and the attacker's arm reaches its full extension, bring your blocking hand across your body allowing your shoulders and torso to rotate slightly, and as you finish your step, your blocking hand should make contact with the soft part of the attacker's forearm and gently brush along the forearm towards the fist.

- Stop brushing along the attacker's forearm when you get to the wrist and leave your blocking hand in place until the attacker removes their arm.

- As soon as the punch has been blocked, the attacker should remove it by allowing the arm to relax and return to a central position ready for whatever is going to happen next.

▶ **Video 31: The Parrot Punch with Opposite-Side Block**

▶ **Video 32: The Cross Parrot Punch with Opposite-Side Block**

## The Crash Block

*'A type of block made by stepping inside the reach of an attack and using both arms to protect the target.'*

The Crash Block can be used to help you get into close distance and move more towards a grab or grapple moment in the fight, or it can simply be a moment of desperation.

You will need to use the soft outside of your forearms when making this block. Both arms are raised together and meet the incoming attack at the same time – not one after the other. The hands can be left open, with thumbs and fingers straight and together, or you can close your fists.

Make sure you start this block from outside of normal distance because not only will the attacker be stepping forwards with the punch, but the victim will also be stepping forwards towards the attacker as they make the block. Be careful not to step into each other and tread on each other's toes or bash knees together.

- Establish eye contact with your partner.

- As the attacker makes their preparation, begin to make your avoidance.

- Step forwards with the foot on the *opposite* side of the body to where the attack is aimed (so step forwards with the right foot if the punch is aimed at the parrot on your left shoulder).

- Begin to raise both arms in front of your body. Keep them close to you and keep the hands above the elbows.

- As the attacker completes their step forwards and finishes the punch, you should turn to face their arm and place the outside of both your forearms against their arm. Be sure to place one arm either side of their elbow joint to help keep them safe.

- Keep your arms close to you and remember not to beat their arm away. It is meant to look as if you stopped their attack in its path.

- The blocking arms should be vertical from the elbow up to the hand and the forearms should be parallel to each other.

- Once the block has been made, the attacker can once again relax their arm and return it to a fighting position or simply get on with whatever is meant to happen next.

Remember that the most important thing about blocking a punch is to move out of the way. It helps to tell the story that you did not want to get punched in the head, but the actual movement of your head away from the punch also helps to blur the picture for the audience so they can't tell that the punch was actually aimed at the parrot on your shoulder and not at your head.

▶ **Video 33: The Parrot Punch with Crash Block**

## Storytelling Through Body Language

I often use the Parrot Punch and blocks as a way of getting my students to think about storytelling and how the use of body language can really help. We always talk about picturisation and incorporating character thoughts and choices into the techniques they are learning, but this is a moment where we specifically look at differences and similarities between *trained* fighters, *untrained* fighters, which character is the better fighter, or who is winning at any given moment.

Let us begin by doing the Parrot Punch and the Same-Side Block. When both characters move about the same distance as each other, and both remain reasonably upright and balanced and neither one is showing a strength or weakness greater than the other, then we can say that at that moment both characters are fairly equal. They are both about as good as each other in terms of how they fight. I call this *neutral* – neither character is better than the other at this moment in the story.

Let us now think about *untrained* fighters. If your character does not know how to fight, or has very little experience of fighting, then the chances are that they will not see the punch coming until it is almost onto them. In which case they have very little time available to do anything and so they will only move a very small distance. They may actually only have time to flinch or jerk their head away and raise their arm.

Notice in these photographs that the punch is still delivered with a vertical fist (holding the bunch of flowers) and that the block is made with the soft fleshy part of the arm so we are still using the idea of Soft on Soft.

Trained fighters, or characters who have lots of fight experience, will usually see the punch coming very early on in its journey and so they will have lots more time to react to it. Does this mean they will move more? No, not necessarily. A trained fighter – a good fighter – will only move as much as they need to in order to achieve whatever they are trying to do.

Because they see the punch coming early, they have time to decide how to respond and then time to do it. Their training will help their brain work really fast and so sometimes things seem almost to happen in slow motion.

So it is possible that the good, trained fighter will decide to step away from their attacker after making the block as a way of signalling that they do not want to engage in violence.

They may chose to step forwards slightly on a diagonal to get up close to the attacker and so intimidate them.

They may want to get close enough so they can hit back. They may choose which side to step to when avoiding the punch depending on what they want to do next. (If you choose this option, please remember that for us it is not real, so make sure that the Parrot Punch is aimed at the parrot on the side the defender is stepping away from.)

A good, trained fighter will always strive to maintain their balance by keeping their knees bent and making sure that their shoulders stay above their hips. The moment you lean forwards (or back) from the waist then you are off-balance and vulnerable.

This is a brief introduction to things that you need to be aware of and need to think about when creating a fight on stage. What you choose to do if your character is a trained fighter is very different to what you may choose to do if they have never been trained.

Make the relevant choices for your character. Do they know how to fight? Do they *want* to fight? How do you communicate that to the audience in the action you perform?

**Summary**

• Make sure you move your head away from the attack.

• Follow the cueing system: Red Light/Green Light.

• Keep the thumbs tucked in when blocking with your hands ('Hospital/No Hospital').

• Soft on Soft when blocking a punch.

• Commit to the attack.

It is quite easy for these punches to feel fake when you are learning them and the first few times you practise. There is an easy way to prevent this: Make sure you know what you are trying to achieve and commit to your action.

As long as you follow the cueing system (Red Light/Green Light) then you and your partner should be safe. Once you are more familiar and comfortable with the technique and the order things happen in, give yourself an objective and a high intention level. Work out your character's emotional connection to the action and the punch will soon feel much more real.

BLOCKING

# Chapter 8: Kicking

Your character does not need to be a martial-arts expert to include a few kicks in your fight. Untrained characters will often use a kick of some description for the simple reason that the leg is longer than the arm, so you do not need to get as close in order to try and kick someone. If you look at any of the fights in the *Bridget Jones* movies you can see how well kicks can be used in a fight between two untrained characters.

There are essentially three different ways of kicking at someone.

## A Snap Kick

Lift the knee and point it towards the target, then flick the foot out towards the target as quickly as possible from the knee and snap it back before replacing the foot on the ground. The attack is made by using the short lever of the lower leg (below the knee) thus reducing the amount of energy in the attacking limb and making it easier to control.

## A Thrust Kick

Lift the knee and point it towards the target, then push the foot out and fully extend the leg. I often use the image of putting my foot against a closed door and pushing it open to help get the right look and feel.

## A Swing Kick

This time the attack is made by swinging the whole leg from the hip joint to maximise the energy in the attack. It is somewhat like kicking a ball. The leg should remain relatively straight throughout the attack as the movement comes from the hip.

▶ **Video 34: The Three Types of Kick**

There are, of course, different types of kick within each category. Let us now have a look at some of them, starting with kicks that are avoided by the victim.

## The Heel Kick

The Heel Kick is a type of Thrust Kick. Imagine you have your arms full (carrying something maybe), and you need to use your foot to open a door and step straight through as it opens.

The story of this attack is that you are driving the heel of your foot forwards in an attempt to smash the victim's hip joint. But they see it coming just in time and they are able to step out of the way of your attack.

This kick travels in a straight line towards the target and it follows the exact same Cue – Reaction – Action sequence, or Red Light/Green Light, as the Parrot Punch described in the previous chapter. In other words, the attacker starts off by showing the attack to the victim, the victim starts to make their avoidance and then the attacker executes the rest of the attack.

We will also be utilising the Displacement of Target concept again, in exactly the same way as we did with the Parrot Punch.

- Start well out of distance from one another.

- Get eye contact with your partner.

- The attacker then looks at the target (just outside the body, level with the victim's hip).

- Prepare the attack by walking into distance and lifting your foot up by raising the knee as high as you can towards your chest. Keep the foot as close to you as you can and show your partner the sole of your foot.

- As the victim, when you see the foot raising up you should begin to make your avoidance.

- Avoid by stepping out to the side, away from where the attack is aimed. It doesn't really matter how you step or move your feet, as long as you are taking the intended target away from the line of the attack. Be sure to maintain your balance as you move.

- Once you see the victim begin their avoidance you can make the attack by straightening the leg and pushing the foot straight forwards towards the target – like pushing open a door.

- The foot should travel in a straight line and as horizontally as you can manage. Avoid driving the foot down into the floor, but push straight through to open the door.

- Once your leg is fully extended in the attack, gravity will bring the foot back to the floor. There is no need to stamp down or think about bringing the foot back towards you. Just let the leg extend and gravity will do the rest for you.

- You should finish the attack in quite a long stance, with the kicking leg bent at the knee and the foot pointing straight forwards and your back leg straight. Keep your body upright to maintain your balance and your weight should be evenly distributed over both feet. This is known as a lunge.

As you get more comfortable and confident with the technique you will naturally want to put more energy into the attack. Always remember that you must lift your knee and foot *first* before driving the foot towards the target. This increased energy as you lift the foot will create a slight hop or jump on your supporting leg which can help communicate how much your character is committed to the action.

If you cannot raise the foot high enough to attack your partner's hip, then feel free to aim at the level of their knee instead. It works in the same way. Just remember that the target is to the *outside* of the knee.

▶ **Video 35: The Same-Side Heel Kick with Avoidance**

You can, of course, aim this kick to the hip or knee on the opposite side of the body – just as you did with the Parrot Punch. Tell your partner where you are going to aim before you begin, so that they can move away from where you aim the kick.

> ▶ **Video 36: The Opposite-Side Heel Kick with Avoidance**

## The Horizontal Swing Kick

The Horizontal Swing Kick sounds a bit like a dance move – something out of a jive routine maybe. But it is just another way of trying to attack your partner from a place of relative safety for your character (i.e. too far away to get hit in the head).

This attack does exactly what it says on the tin. It travels in the horizontal plane and it is a Swing Kick, so the leg stays relatively straight and the whole leg moves from the hip joint.

We follow the same Red Light/Green Light system to help keep us safe and we can still work out of distance.

This attack can be performed to many different targets. It depends on where you are, where the intended victim is, how high you can lift your leg, what the story demands, and so on. For the sake of describing how to do it, I am simply going to imagine that attacker and victim are facing each other and that the attack is aimed at waist height on the victim – in other words, you are trying to kick them in the stomach or the floating ribs.

* Start out of distance – far enough away so you can't actually kick your partner.

* Get eye contact with them to make sure they are ready and to tell them you are ready.

* Look at the target which in this instance is their stomach area or their waist.

114

- Make your preparation by stepping forwards on the non-kicking foot and planting it firmly to give you stability. Keep it slightly turned out as well to allow you to turn your hips in the attack and swing your kicking foot all the way around.

- Finish the preparation by raising the kicking leg out to the side of you slightly. The knee can be slightly bent and the foot should be pointed, as if you are trying to kick with the top part of the foot or the laces section of your shoe.

- As soon as the victim sees the attacker's leg being raised in preparation for the attack, you should begin your avoidance.

- Jump backwards away from the attacker and pull your hips and your stomach back out of the way of the kick. Raise your hands up above your head to keep them out of the line of the attacker's foot – there is no point not getting kicked in the stomach if you just get kicked in the arms instead!

- As soon as the attacker sees the victim start their avoidance you should complete the kick.

- Swing from the hip, keeping the leg as straight as you can (or as straight as you want).

- Continue to raise the foot until it is at the height of the victim's stomach/waist, then keep it swinging horizontally right the way across to the other side of the body.

- Try to get the kicking foot up to the correct height before it crosses in front of the body so the attack is clear and horizontal as it passes across the intended target area. This also helps your partner avoid it correctly, tell the right story and make you both look good on stage.

- As the attacking foot swings past the target and loses momentum, gravity will naturally bring it back down to the ground.

▶ **Video 37: The Horizontal Swing Kick**

As with the Heel Kick, if you can't get your leg high enough to attack at stomach/waist height, then there is absolutely no reason why you cannot make this attack at the knee instead. It would work in the same way – you could even perform the same kind of avoidance, or you could simply pull the relevant leg out of the way of the attack instead.

There are lots of possibilities with this. All you have to do is communicate with your partner and decide between you what is going to happen. Then, once you are both clear about what you are doing, you can work out how best to tell the story to the audience.

## Non-contact Kicks

Remember that a non-contact strike is defined as 'A blow delivered with the illusion of contact, properly masked from the audience, with a well timed knap.' So for the next techniques we need to be aware of where we are on stage so we can create the proper illusion for the audience.

When performing non-contact kicks we need to be out of distance again. Just remember that your legs are longer than your arms so you need to be further apart than you would be for a non-contact punch. As you practise these kicks, feel free to start off by measuring out the right distance. My legs may be longer than yours so what is the right distance for you may well be too close for me. Check by simply extending your leg to the target and making sure you can't actually reach it. Then, as you rehearse, you and your partner will start to see and gauge the right distance for you. This just takes a bit of practice and patience.

### The Stomach Kick

For a Stomach Kick we need the victim standing downstage with their back to the audience. The attacker will be upstage of them and approaching on a slight diagonal so they can be seen.

Which side the attacker comes from depends on and also determines which leg they are going to kick with.

Right-leg kick

Left-leg kick

If you want to kick with your right leg then you should approach from the right-hand side of the victim – in other words from upstage-left of the victim (see left-hand picture, above).

If you are approaching from the upstage-right angle then you should kick with your left leg (see right-hand picture, above).

As always, start by getting eye contact with your partner then look to the target. As with the Stomach Punch described earlier, the target for this kick is the magic line that travels directly upstage from the victim's stomach roughly twelve to eighteen inches away from the body.

This particular kick is a Snap Kick and you should be kicking with the ball of the foot. So extend your foot and try to curl the toes up into the same position as they would be if you were standing on your tip toes.

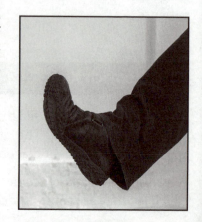

- Step into the attack as you did with the Heel Kick and plant your supporting foot firmly on the ground.
- Lift the knee of your attacking leg and aim it towards the target.

- Flicking from the knee, send the kicking foot out directly towards the target, making sure you reach the magic line. Present the ball of the foot as much as you can (footwear allowing) as this is the part of your foot you are meant to be striking with.

- Make sure the foot flicks out to the height of the stomach to meet the magic line. If your foot is not high enough it will look like you have kicked them somewhere different.

- As soon as the foot reaches the magic line, snap it back away from the victim's stomach and place it back on the ground in front of you.

- At the moment the foot reaches the line, you can make the knap on your upstage thigh. Try to keep the overall movement of the knapping hand small and natural to hide it from the audience.

As the victim you should react at the moment the attacker's foot lines up with your stomach. This will be the moment it hits the magic line, and hopefully the same time as the knap is made.

Your reaction will be the same as for the Stomach Punch described earlier, but you will want to make it a slightly larger reaction this time because the kick is a stronger attack than the punch.

- Pull the stomach in quickly and allow your lower spine to curve and push out behind you.

- Pull your shoulders up and forwards to emphasise the arch in the back.

- Keep your head and shoulders above the level of your hips.

- Make a loud vocal sound as if the air has been forced out of your body and your lungs. This will augment the knap made by the attacker and help convince the audience that you have really been hit.

You may even want to bring your hands towards your stomach in your reaction, but make sure this only happens *after* the attack has been made.

▶ **Video 38: The Stomach Kick**

## The Head Kick (with Victim Kneeling)

There are different ways of performing the Head Kick. You could execute it as a Snap Kick (which is how we will look at it in a moment), or you could do it as a Swing Kick. If you are particularly flexible and can get your foot high enough, then your victim can remain standing. Or they can simply be on their knees as if something has already happened in the scene or the fight to lower them to this position. That is how I suggest you start off.

We will, therefore, place our victim in the same downstage position as for the Stomach Kick, but kneeling rather than standing up. When you kneel it is important to kneel up with your shoulders, hips and knees all aligned above each other, rather than slumping back to kneel on your ankles.

As the attacker, begin to one side of the victim, approaching from the same side as the foot you want to kick with (i.e. approach from the victim's right-hand side if you want to kick with your right foot, or their left-hand side to kick with your left foot). You should be kicking with your upstage leg.

Make sure you are at right angles to the victim as you approach. As they are facing directly upstage, you should be facing directly across the stage.

You must also make sure your distance is correct. If you stand too far upstage of the victim then the audience will not believe the illusion. Stand too close and the results could be horrific!

Ideally, you should be at a distance where you can walk past the victim without touching them. As you walk past there should be just a few inches between your downstage arm and their body. Remember that you are going to kick with the upstage leg – that's the leg furthest away from the victim, so this spacing will help keep things safe.

One final thing before I describe the technique. I would suggest that you do *not* try to get eye contact with your partner before you perform this technique for two reasons.

First, as the victim, you need to be looking straight ahead of you for this to work. If you look at the attacker, then turn back to look straight ahead, it can seem a bit odd and distracting.

Second, as the attacker, the more eye contact you get here from the victim, the more likely you are to allow the kicking foot to drift in towards their face which will get scary and dangerous.

We do want to give the attacker some kind of signal to say that the victim is ready, though. So I am simply going to suggest that once the victim is ready to perform their reaction and they know what is about to happen, then that is the moment for them to kneel up into the required position and look ahead.

For example, maybe something happened to make you fall over (a trip, a punch). Act that moment until you are ready to perform your reaction to being kicked in the head, then kneel up to show the attacker you are ready. Then – and only then – will they execute the attack.

When you are both ready and in the right positions and at the correct distance then you can proceed with the Head Kick.


## The Action

The action is the attacker's movement.

- Look at the target. This is the spot on the magic line from the victim's face that is also in front of you.

- Step in towards the victim and plant your downstage foot firmly to give you stability.

- Raise the knee of your kicking leg (upstage leg) as high as you can. Really try to bring it in towards your chest. The higher you can lift your knee, the higher the kick will go.

- Point your foot. With this kick you are supposedly kicking with the top of your foot (the laces area of your shoe). This is simply to help the foot be as long as possible so that it can cross the line more effectively and therefore create the illusion of contact.

- Flick from the knee and send the foot out and up until it crosses the line at the point of the target.

Make sure you keep looking at the space in front of the victim's head (the target) when you are kicking. This will help you to keep your hips and torso square on and perpendicular to the victim and ensure that your kicking foot does not drift in towards their face. This is more than a little important!

You could have the victim make the knap as an alternative – a Chest Knap could work well.

## The Reaction

As with all reactions, timing is important. So, as the victim, make sure you are looking in front of you so you can see the attacker's foot cross the line. When you see it go past your face then you can react.

- Start in the position described above, kneeling up with your shoulders, hips and knees aligned vertically above each other.

- Look straight ahead along the magic line.

- Tilt your head up and back as if you are looking at something running up the wall in front of you and onto the ceiling. This should help to keep the back of your neck as long as you can to avoid injury.

- Hunch your shoulders to provide a cushion at the base of your neck for extra protection.

- You may want to bring your hands up to your face to help tell the story of pain and injury.

- Start to look over your shoulder, away from the attacker. This will naturally turn your head and upper body away from them as if you have been kicked.

You may also wish to fall back onto the ground so think back to Chapter 4: Falling and remind yourself how to land. Find your soft padded parts, avoid landing on boney bits, and definitely do not use your hands to brace yourself.

This fall will be very similar to the Fainting Fall we looked at, the main difference is that you start on your knees.

- As you look over your shoulder away from the attacker, check to make sure the area you are going into is clear and safe.

- Push your hips out to the side as you start to present your buttock to land on.

- Reach out with that same-side arm and then place the buttock onto the floor.

- Lay out onto your side along the floor, keeping the arm extended to provide a soft cushion for your head.

- You want to end laying along the floor in a diagonal line backwards from where you were when you were kicked.

As the victim lays themselves out across the floor, and the attacker steps down after performing the kick, the attacker should end up standing above the victim looking down at them.

▶ Video 39: The Head Kick (with Victim Kneeling)

## The Head Kick (with Victim Lying Down)

If the victim is already stretched out on the ground, then there are a few differences in how to perform the technique.

First of all, you will kick with the leg that is nearest the victim – your downstage leg.

Secondly, you should make it a Swing Kick instead of a Snap Kick. So it actually becomes rather like kicking a ball.

Positioning on stage is important again. The victim will be laid out along the floor, but with their head and shoulders raised up slightly. Use the lower arm to support yourself and help push you up from the ground a little.

KICKING

Make sure your body is in a relatively straight line so that your knees and arms don't get in the way of the attacker's foot as they kick. And try to keep your head in line with your body rather than sticking it forwards and making it easier for the attacker to kick it accidentally.

The direction in which you lie dictates which foot the attacker can kick with. In the photograph above we are looking at the victim from an upstage position (their back is facing the audience). This means that their head is aiming towards stage left and their feet to stage right. With the victim in this position the attacker *must* approach from stage right and kick with the right foot. If the attacker needs or wants to kick with their left foot, then the victim must lie down with their head on the other side of the stage, but still keeping their back to the audience (see below).

We can – and indeed should – establish eye contact with our partner before executing this technique. So once both of you are in the right positions and you have established eye contact then you can proceed.

## The Action

- The attacker approaches from the feet end of the victim. Make your approach at a slight angle rather than absolutely parallel to the victim.

- Look at the target – again this is the magic line running directly upstage from the victim's face. Pick a spot about twelve inches along the line upstage from their head.

- Plant your upstage leg firmly to give you the stability you need and prepare the kick by drawing the downstage leg back. Remember this is going to be a Swing Kick (like kicking a ball) so keep the leg relatively straight and make the movement from the hip joint.

- Now swing from the hip and propel the kicking foot forwards past the victim's face to make sure you cross the line.

KICKING

- The foot should travel in a slight arc or a curved trajectory. As the foot is crossing the line it should be starting to curve and travel away from the victim.

- As you swing your leg, keep the foot pointed with the toes turned in very slightly so that you are almost presenting the outside edge of the foot.

- As the foot passes the victim's face you should knap using your upstage hand on your upstage thigh. This can be a slightly bigger move than before because the kick is a much bigger action in general, and the knap will be hidden in the natural swing and movement of your arm as you deliver the kick.

- As your leg reaches the natural end of its full swing (keeping it on the arc away from the victim's face), just step down to finish the attack. You may find that your supporting leg hops or skips a little as you swing the kick. This is normal and is simply due to the energy you put into the attack.

## The Reaction

The Head Kick, with the victim lying on the floor, is probably the biggest and most aggressive attack we have looked at in this book. And it is almost certain that your character would be rendered unconscious (at least!) by a kick to the head of this nature – so you are going to end up sprawled across the floor.

The good news is you are already lying on the floor so it should be fairly straightforward. Just remember to avoid slamming elbows and other boney parts of your body into the floor, and to protect your head.

- After you have established eye contact with the attacker, shift your focus and look at their foot as it prepares and then travels through the attack.

- When you see their foot go past your face, lift your head up, reaching back from the crown of your head. Try to keep the neck aligned with the upper spine.

- Push your hips forwards and your shoulders backwards to arch through your back. This will help to increase the size of your reaction without having to put unnecessary strain on the neck.

- Bring your head and body back to a neutral alignment once more as you bring your hands to your face and roll over onto your back.

- Make sure you rotate enough to land on the muscle group around your shoulder blade area rather than landing heavily on the point of the shoulder itself.

The video for this technique also shows an alternative reaction which involves rotating along your body's long axis and bringing the upper shoulder forwards and underneath you. This has the advantage of leaving the victim facing the audience.

▶ **Video 40: The Head Kick (with Victim Lying Down)**

## Dramatising the Kicks

When thinking about the performance of these kicks, you must remember that the leg is a much bigger and stronger limb than the arm, and the foot is larger than the fist. So the kick is a bigger, stronger attack than the punches or slaps we looked at earlier. This fact must be represented when you dramatise the kicks – by making your characters acknowledge the greater level of violence or risk or danger they face.

Even with the avoided kicks what the audience wants to see is the very real danger that the victim is in and their fear of getting hit by this attack. What are the consequences to your character if that

Heel Kick actually 'hits' its intended target? Will that mean you lose the fight? What happens if you lose the fight?

If you are the character making the attack, why do you choose to kick instead of punch? Is it because you are further away from your intended victim and can't reach them with your fist? Or is it a *Bridget Jones* situation where you don't know how to fight, you are afraid of what might happen and so you stay as far away as possible?

We have talked about intention levels before, and I encourage you again to use the scale of 1 to 10 when trying to find the right intention level for each attack. Not everything will be an intention level of 8 or 9. Especially if you are increasing the fear factor and decreasing the fighting ability of your character, then the intention level of each attack may be tempered somewhat by that fear. Maybe.

These are choices you have to make. So go ahead and make them early in your rehearsal period so that you give them time to evolve and develop – maybe change them if they start to feel wrong. Then you can really start to act the fight rather than just present it.

KICKING

### Summary

- Increase your distance to allow for the extra length of your leg.
- Be clear which type of kick you are using (Swing, Thrust or Snap Kick).
- Remember which part of the foot you are kicking with.
- Keep a strong thought in your head about what you are trying to do to the victim.
- Reactions must be bigger for kicks than for punches.

Kicks are a great way to add a bit of variety and interest into a fight, but remember that few characters are trained in martial arts, so you need to choose your kicks carefully.

You also need to choose when and how to include them. They can be a great way of getting in closer to your partner so that you can punch them. Alternatively, to keep someone far away from you. But if they land, they are usually going to finish the fight. *Especially* if it is a kick to the head.

# Chapter 9: Playing Pain

Nobody comes out of a fight without having been hurt in some way. Every moment of violence causes some form of pain to someone. Any fight on stage where the actors do not show us that they have been hurt is unrealistic and less interesting for the audience. Let's face it, even Superman showed pain.

To engage the audience and help them buy into the illusions you are creating you must have your characters acknowledge and respond to the injuries they have suffered and the pain they feel as a result of them.

This chapter is about helping you find a way to express that injury and pain so that the audience can recognise and understand it. It will provide you with a way in, as it were. It is not intended as an exhaustive and definitive rule book, merely as a means of starting you thinking about some of the things you need to be working on in order to portray your character's story as fully and truthfully as you can.

If *you* (not your character, but the real you) were in a fight or got injured in some way, you would be able to answer the following questions:

- Where does it hurt?

- How much does it hurt?

- What kind of pain is it?

- What damage has been done to you?

- Does it have any physical effect on how you move or speak?

If *you* would be able to answer these questions, then you need to answer each of them for your character too.

## Where Does It Hurt?

Fairly obviously, it hurts in the place where your character has been struck, but it might also include other areas. For example, if you get punched in the head then the point of impact would hurt, but so too might your neck due to the violent and sudden stress it has been subjected to when your head is forced to move.

Make your answer to this question as specific and as detailed as possible. If you have been punched in the face, the answer to this first question is not 'My face', but is more accurately: 'The cheekbone on the right side of my face just below the corner of my eye socket.' Or maybe: 'My lower jawbone on the left side of my face and the teeth inside my mouth and the inside of my cheek.'

The more specific and detailed you can make your answer, the more detailed and interesting your story will become – and the more realistic and believable it will be for the audience.

You should also find that the more detail you can put into your answer to this question, the more it will help you provide details for the other questions and vice versa.

## How Much Does It Hurt?

There are several factors that will help you answer this question. How young and strong is your character? How strong is the character that has just hit you? Is your character physically larger than the other character or are you much smaller? Was it a solid hit or a glancing blow? Do they have fight training or fight experience? Do *you*? Have you ever been hit before? Where on your person were you hit? What were you hit with? Were you already carrying an injury in the place you have just been hit?

You should also bear in mind that each type of attack can be graded. I like to think of the attacks sitting on different rungs of a ladder. The higher the ladder you go, the bigger and more powerful the attack. So, for example, a Profile Slap could be placed on quite a low rung of the ladder. A non-contact kick to the head will be significantly higher up the ladder. A Jab Punch may be higher than an Upstage/Downstage Slap, but lower than the Cross Punch.

When thinking about how much something hurts, I encourage actors to use a scale of 1 to 10 again, where 1 represents 'I barely felt it' and 10 represents the worst, most intense pain you can possibly imagine. This is a similar idea to the scales used for determining the level of intention that we first explored back in Chapter 1.

Your job is to decide what rung of the ladder the attack is on, and match the level of pain to that attack, bearing in mind the other circumstances mentioned above and the attacker's level of intention.

## What Kind of Pain Is It?

This is exactly the kind of question your doctor would ask you. Your answer should be a descriptive word. Here are a few examples that my own students have come up with in classes over the years:

| | | |
|---|---|---|
| • Stinging | • Constant | • Crippling |
| • Burning | • Intermittent | • Deadening |
| • Throbbing | • Sudden | • Slicing |
| • Stabbing | • Blinding | • Overwhelming |
| • Shooting | • Cramping | • Ringing |
| • Piercing | • Niggling | • Sickening |
| • Sharp | • Crashing | • Breathtaking |
| • Dull | • Tearing | • Constricting |

Different types of injury will suggest different types of pain. Make your choice as appropriate and honest as you can. Think back to any injuries you may have received in the past and see if they might bear any resemblance to the injury your character is receiving now. If you have ever hit your own thumb with a hammer, you might be able to remember that feeling and use it to determine how it feels for your character to get punched in the side of the head. To help you answer this important question and choose your own adjective to describe the pain, it will help you to know what damage has been done and what kind of injury your character has sustained.

## What Damage Has Been Done to You?

If you get punched in the stomach, you may not receive any significant injury other than being winded (which you would know due to your lack of breath and the difficulty you have taking more air into your lungs) – and maybe a bruise developing.

If you receive a Jab Punch to the face, the consequences may be more severe. Does your nose break? Do you feel and hear it crack? Do your eyes fill up with tears? Do you momentarily get a bright white light filling your vision and preventing you from seeing? Does your nose start to bleed?

You are the actor so you must make the effort to answer these questions for your character. Here are a few different types of injury that could be sustained in an unarmed fight, along with ideas of what type of action may cause them.

- **Contusion** (a bruise) – blunt force blow of some sort such as a punch or kick.

- **Abrasion** (a graze) – falling over and skinning your knees or hands.

- **Fracture** (of a bone) – many possible causes, including falling, a wrist lock, a kick or punch. Fractures can be open or closed. An open fracture is where the bone sticks out through the skin, a closed fracture is where the skin is not broken.

- **Asphyxia** (difficulty breathing) or **hypoxia** (lack of oxygen) – from strangulation.

- **Crush injuries** – can lead to fractures and internal injuries. Possible from strangulation, when the windpipe gets crushed.

- **Concussion** – from any blow to the head which causes the brain to shake around inside the skull. If the blow is serious enough it could even result in **compression** (bleeding inside the skull).

- **Laceration** (ripping of the skin) – possible from a slap or punch especially if the attacker was weaing a ring. Could be internal (cheek being ripped open against your teeth).

## Does It Have Any Physical Effect on How You Move or Speak?

Now that you have figured out what attack has been made, where it has hurt you, what damage has been done, what type of pain it is and the level of pain you experience, you need to think about how it affects you.

A kick to the stomach may knock the wind out of you and possibly cause some internal damage. It would almost certainly have you doubled over at least for a while. You may be clutching your abdomen to try and ease the pain. This will have a direct impact on how you can move. You certainly won't be able to walk around normally holding yourself up straight. At least not for a while. So that quick exit you had planned may need to be rethought to allow you to be honest about the pain your character is carrying with them at that moment. You would also have difficulty speaking because you are winded, so that lovely forty-line monologue you have right after taking the kick suddenly needs to be delivered differently and with a different energy and rhythm to it.

## How Much Pain to Play

Are you really supposed to convey all of this pain in the middle of a fight? This is a very good question. Do you have time between getting punched on the nose and then thrown to the ground and strangled to play the pain and effects of the punch? Well, the answer is no... and yes.

Clearly the time taken between each action of the fight is limited, so you can't spend very long showing us how much pain you are in when that nasty person broke your cheekbone just below your left eye.

But in a real-life fight – a highly stressful situation – the body produces adrenaline and other hormones which prepare the body for the 'fight or flight' response. Adrenaline also acts as a natural painkiller. It basically prevents us feeling the effects of any injuries until we are out of the stressful situation of the fight. So we could take a punch to the head and not really feel its effects until much later on.

This can get a bit boring on stage, however, so we need to find a happy medium that helps you tell the story to the audience whilst maintaining the reality of what is happening to your character. You must show the audience the moment of the hit and show them that you have been hurt, but then we need to see you put that pain to one side whilst you continue dealing with the situation at hand until it's over and your brain then has a chance to remind you that any injuries really do hurt and this is what pain feels like! Then you can really put into action all that work you have done on the type of injury you have sustained and what pain level you experience. That is when it gets fun.

Adrenaline also heightens our awareness of what is happening. Our brain seems to work much faster than normal and things appear to be happening in slow motion. So although things may happen in the blink of an eye, in our head it may seem like a couple of minutes. This allows us to acknowledge what has happened and how it feels before the next thing happens.

When you are fighting on stage you need to show us the moment you get hurt, then focus on what is coming next and play that part of the story. When the fight is over, or when there is a pause, you can come back to the injuries you have received and remind us that you are in pain. Pain does not just happen and then disappear. It will come back – sometimes with a vengeance. The more you can refer back to the pain and let the audience see how it has affected you, the more they will engage with you and what you are going through. If you don't carry that pain and injury with you then your story becomes false and less interesting.

Some moments of violence are just that. Isolated moments. You get slapped. No big fight, just the one action. How much pain you experience, how long it stays with you and how it affects what you do or say next may not be as great as what happens to you in a big bar-room punch-up – indeed the effects may be more psychological rather than physical – but you still need to work out the answers and fill your story with as much detail as you can.

## The Sounds of Violence

Having worked out what injury you have received, how much it hurts, what type of pain you feel and so on, there is one thing left to do and that is work out how to express all of that to the audience. Yes, a lot of this is down to how you react, how you move, how you screw your face up and show us your agony. But the one thing that really carries all the way to the back of the auditorium is your voice and the sounds you make. Think of this as part of the soundtrack to the fight. Even silent movies had some form of musical accompaniment to help the audience connect with what they were watching. We also need to help the audience connect with what they are watching by engaging them aurally as well as visually.

I am not going to try and tell you *how* to make the sounds, but I am going to suggest ways of choosing which sounds to make and how you can vary your choices to make the sounds you create more appropriate and more interesting.

The only technical advice I would give you is to keep your jaw and throat as relaxed as you can, so the sounds are as free as possible and do not harshly impact on your vocal folds. (Don't forget, you may need to deliver that long monologue at the end of your fight!) If you have any doubts or concerns then contact a qualified voice teacher who will be able to help you in the production of the sounds you choose.

If you make the same sound for every occasion that you get hit, or for every time you make an attack, it becomes very boring very quickly. Here are a few ideas on how to vary the sounds you make to keep the music of the fight as exciting as the fight itself.

There are five different things on which you need to decide when working out what sounds to use to represent your pain:

- Which vowel sound you use.
- How loud you make it.
- How long the sound lasts for.
- What pitch the sound should be at (high note or low note).
- Whether to make the sound on an in-breath or an out-breath.

## Vowel Sound

Try avoiding the use of the traditional 'Ah' or 'Uh' sounds too much. Sure, they can be very useful, but experiment with different vowel sounds too. Be bold and daring in your choices. Try the unexpected – sometimes that can make the audience believe it more because it's a sound they were not expecting to hear so they think it must be real. And try to avoid saying the words 'Ow' or 'Ouch' unless they are actually scripted. Use your rehearsal period to play around and try different things until you settle on sounds that work for you in that particular moment.

## Volume

Vary how loud each sound is. Of course we want the people at the back of the auditorium to hear everything, but not every attack will land with the same force and cause the same level of pain, so we should experiment with a different volume. Find the hits and injuries that *really* hurt and work out when it would be appropriate to make a sound for that, and then decide how loud to make the sound.

In with this, you should also consider whether to make the sound a voiced sound or an unvoiced sound. The easiest way I can describe these (if you are unfamiliar with the terms) is that a voiced sound is like you are speaking aloud whereas an unvoiced sound is like a whisper.

## Duration

Some sounds will be long and drawn out; others will be very short and even curtailed in some way. It may even be that the attack stops whatever sound you were making rather than causing you to make another sound. It's always worth trying different options, but make sure you remain truthful and make sure the sounds you make match the situation.

## Pitch

Being hit in different places on your body will mean you need to produce sounds in different areas of your vocal register (sometimes a low note or a higher one).

As a general rule, the closer to your physical centre the attack hits, the lower in pitch the sound will be. The closer to your extremities you get hit then the higher pitch the sound will be. So hitting your thumb with a hammer or stubbing your toe on the edge of the door will create a higher-sounding note than getting hit in your gut.

## In- or Out-Breath

You must also decide whether it's right to make the sound as you exhale or when you inhale. Being punched in the stomach will almost certainly result in a sound made on an out-breath because one effect of the punch is to drive the air out of your body. But if you slice your finger open on a piece of paper it is quite often a sharp intake of breath that produces the sound, possibly sucked in between your teeth. If you stub your toe hard on the door frame it might be a combination – a short, sharp intake of breath followed by a long, loud groan on the out-breath.

### Summary

• Audiences love to see characters in pain, so give it to them.

• Be as specific and detailed as you can.

• Work out how the injury or pain affects your movement.

• Be bold with your choices and be willing to experiment.

• Start to rehearse your vocal sounds as early as possible.

You now have a lot of things to think about: What attack have you just received, where did it land, what damage has been done to you, how much does it hurt, what type of pain is it, what type of sound do you need to make to represent that pain, and when should you make that sound? Many times, these answers can come fairly instinctively and it is quite straightforward to reach your decisions. If you get slapped you can probably create an appropriate sound to go with that fairly easily and quickly without really thinking about it. But maybe, just maybe, you could make it even more convincing for the audience if you change one or two things about that sound such as the pitch or whether it's made on an in-breath instead of an out-breath, or whether it's a voiced or unvoiced sound. If you are involved in a longer fight then varying the sounds you use for different moments will significantly increase the believability of your fight, as well as the audience's enjoyment of it. So go ahead and use your rehearsal time to experiment and see what you come up with.

PLAYING PAIN

146

# Chapter 10:
# Fighting

## Starting Points

Let me be perfectly frank here. Creating your own fight sequence is not easy – especially for someone who has little or no experience of how to fight and how to do it safely. So the first and possibly most important thing to say here is: '*Know when you need to call in a professional.*'

Hopefully this book has given you a good understanding of how to keep moments of aggression safe and how to make them look believable for your audience. If you are working in amateur theatre, a fringe venue somewhere, or maybe at college or university, then I hope that this book will give you the knowledge you need to safely stage and perform acts of violence.

But staging the moment when Lord Capulet slaps his daughter because she does not want to marry Paris is one thing. Staging the opening brawl in the same play with a cast of ten or twenty people is something else entirely. There are so many other things to take into consideration. That is the job of the professional fight director. For the sake of everyone's health and enjoyment, know your limits and don't be afraid to call in professional help. It is not always as expensive as you might think, and it is always cheaper than the potential law suit and compensation payments that may arise if you don't.

Let us assume that you have a moment in your play that requires a fight or struggle of some sort. A moment to further the story where two characters get aggressive with each other for some reason. Where do you start? How do you plan what to do? Here are some of the things that a fight director will always have in mind when creating a fight.

## Objectives

Start with finding out what the fight (or moment of violence) is meant to *achieve*. Why has the author included it in the play at this particular moment? What is it meant to say about the characters involved? Is it meant to shut someone up or is it to show that one character has lost control? Is it more deliberate and calculated than that? Is it the characters' way of asserting their authority over one another? What are the characters' objectives within the fight and within the scene?

## Character History

You need to understand what kind of people are involved in the fight. Are they trained fighters as Mercutio and Tybalt undoubtedly would be? Or are they inexperienced and ignorant of fighting styles and techniques as Amanda and Elyot are likely to be in Noël Coward's *Private Lives*? Have these characters ever fought before and, if so, what was the result? It will certainly affect the choices they make this time if they have previously been beaten up badly by the same character.

## Triggers

These are the moments in the text that propel the character into the moment of violence. It is the thing that is said or done that makes one character attack the other. You must find these moments in the text and use them to justify where the violence is coming from. It is very rare that people will fight or engage in violence towards another person for absolutely no reason. Everything you put on the stage should be justified by what is written in the text.

## Suitability

If the character is a trained, experienced pugilist, it will make sense to have them throw lots of punches rather than kicking out or trying to strangle their antagonist. It makes sense for Lord Capulet to slap Juliet, but if he turned round and punched her in the face we would feel completely differently about him.

Above all, please do not just choose a technique because you think it looks cool. It won't.

# Staging Your Own Fight Sequence

Now that we have talked a little about the theoretical side of planning a fight on stage, what kind of things do you need to think about when actually putting the fight together?

## Keep It Simple

Do only enough in the fight to tell the story – and no more. This will also make it easier for the actors to remember, give them more confidence and keep them safe. From that will come more convincing performances.

## Positioning on Stage

Make sure the actors are in the correct position on stage to make the technique work. Alternatively, choose a technique that works for the positioning you have the actors in. An Upstage/Downstage Slap looks rubbish when performed with the actors in profile to the audience. So either choose the Profile Slap or find a natural way to move the actors into the upstage/downstage position. Always pay attention to the distance between them for each technique.

## Linking More Than One Technique

Going from one technique to another requires some careful rehearsal. Make sure the actors are able to get eye contact between moves – or at least signal and see in some way that they are ready to continue. And make sure the next target is logical and available. For example, if you punch someone in the stomach and they double over, you could follow that by kicking them in the head, but it wouldn't make sense to try the Jab Punch or the Roundhouse Punch because their head is not in the right place for those attacks to work or make sense. If you want to use those techniques, you need to move the victim into a logical position – maybe by grabbing them by the shoulders or standing them upright again before trying to throw the punch.

## Listen to the Actors

Remember that the actors are the people who will have to rehearse this fight over and over again. And they are the ones who will have to perform it on stage. If they say that an action, or a transition between actions, is awkward then you need to find a way of changing it. If it feels awkward then it probably isn't natural or logical for the way their body wants to move and they will have great trouble remembering it. At best, you will have a moment on stage where they forget what they are meant to be doing. At worst, they will do it wrong and someone will get hurt. So listen to what they are saying. If you are the actor and it feels awkward then make sure you say something – it is not just your fellow actors' safety on the line but your own.

Your choices should always tell a story that suits the drama. Those choices should be based on textual evidence and actor choices regarding the characters. Otherwise it becomes 'fight porn'.

## Keeping It Safe

Your choices must always be safe for the actors involved. Not only must the individual techniques be safe for actors to perform (hopefully this book can help you achieve that), but you should also be aware of the actors' own ability levels. An actor with vast amounts of training in stage combat and regular experience performing fights can often perform techniques and sequences that are more complex and demanding. Someone who has no experience should not be encouraged to try the same things without professional supervision. Know your actors and what their limitations are.

Being safe is not just about keeping the right distance, aiming at the right target, getting eye contact at the right moment, staying balanced. It is also about sustainability. Is this actor able to repeat this technique consistently night after night for the duration of the run? And can they do it without endangering themselves or anyone else? If the answer is 'No', then you need to change what they are doing, get rid of it completely, or call for professional help from a fight director.

Keep it simple, keep it safe – and you may just keep it fun!

## Keeping a Record

Before you can rehearse you need to record the fight. Film it on a smartphone or tablet by all means. Ask the stage manager or production assistant to write it down. I would always advise that the actors involved should write it down themselves, regardless of who else is recording it. It helps them to remember the fight.

There are many different ways of writing down a fight and each method has its own particular merits. Ultimately, it does not matter *how* you write it down as long as you can understand what you have written, and continue to do what it says you should be doing.

Personally, I use a version where I divide the page into two columns. I write all my moves in one column and all my partner's moves in the other column. Corresponding moves for my partner and myself will be on the same line but in opposite columns. For example, if I am performing the Upstage/Downstage Slap then I write that down in my column. In the same line of the second column will be written my partner's reaction for the moment I perform the slap (they react and execute a Clap Knap.)

| My Moves | Partner's Moves |
|---|---|
| RH Upstage/Downstage Slap | React & Clap Knap |
| Avoid and LH Same-Side Block | RH Parrot Punch to Left Parrot |

The second line above shows that my partner performs a Parrot Punch with their right hand towards the parrot on *my* left shoulder. My corresponding move is to avoid the punch and perform a Same-Side Block with my left hand.

This method helps me keep track of what is happening and when. It also clearly shows that everything I do is related or connected to something my partner does. A good reminder that this is a team effort – a partnership. We are working together to tell a story.

## When to Rehearse

Once it is recorded, make sure you rehearse your fight sequence as often as you can. How often you need to rehearse will vary from production to production and from person to person. If you just have one slap, or a push and a fall, then make time to rehearse the action in isolation each time you rehearse the scene. Just take a few minutes to walk through the action on its own to make sure that everyone is still happy with what they are doing. Then you can rehearse it as part of the scene with appropriate acting and emotions. If the actor is having difficulty, then either change what they are being asked to do or give them more time to practise outside of the scene rehearsal. Give them ten minutes at every rehearsal if they need the time to get it right and not hurt themselves or anyone else.

If it is a longer or more complex sequence, then you need to schedule specific rehearsal time. This may be every day (or every day that you rehearse), or it may be once a week. The frequency of rehearsal will depend on the length and complexity of the sequence, as well as the experience and ability of the performers. The more time you give to rehearsing the fight, the more confident the actors will be and the more likely they are to remain safe and give a convincing performance.

During the run of the show you should also schedule a fight call before every performance. This is a specific rehearsal for all moments of violence in the show and is held as close to the half-hour call as possible. It is a chance for the cast to go through the fights and actions before the show to make sure they can remember what they are doing and to work out any issues that may have arisen from the previous night's performance.

In the fight call, run each moment three times. Once at walking pace to mark through the sequence of moves. Then a second time at about half speed to get the rhythms and timings going again. Then do it one last time with about three-quarters of the energy level you will use in performance.

If the fight is after the interval, then allow the actors to find a space backstage somewhere at the interval to slowly mark it through again.

This fight call should be held before the first performance each day. Your stage manager, or whoever has been appointed the person responsible for the fight, should run the fight call.

## How to Rehearse

You should aim to set the choreography as early in the rehearsal period as you can. This will maximise the time the actors have in which to get really familiar with the moves and to find their intention levels and their own natural pace at which to perform the fight.

Everyone will have a different pace at which they can fight. 'How fast should it be?' is a question that is almost impossible to answer. It will be as fast as it needs to be for these actors to play their objectives and tell the story as truthfully as they can. If they truly engage in the situation their character is in, if they commit to the action both physically and emotionally, and if they achieve the appropriate intention level, then that will give them the pace they need in that moment. This is usually referred to as 'performance pace'.

When rehearsing, performance pace should always be your final goal not your starting point. Begin by working slowly. Give yourself a chance to think about what you are doing and make sure you are doing it correctly. Working slowly allows actors to remain safe while they are still learning the sequence. It gives them a good opportunity to make sure their balance is good and that they are maintaining a good distance between each other so that any slaps and punches remain safe. Working slowly allows them to recognise and control the moments when they need to change from being out of distance for an upstage/downstage technique to being in distance for a profile technique.

It also forces them to breathe. Breathing is vital in a fight because it helps you stay relaxed and keeps a steady flow of oxygen going to the brain, which means you can think clearly about what you are doing.

Use these slow rehearsals to think about incorporating all the work you have done on the pain and injuries sustained by your character. Build in the moments of vocalisation now and they will become natural and instinctive by the time you reach performance.

If your action involves one moment of violence, such as a slap, then you can work up to performance pace fairly soon. Once both actors are confident with all aspects of the movement and they have a good control over their balance and their distance, then they should be allowed to start finding their natural pace and rhythm for that moment.

But if your fight is longer and progresses from a slap into a more sustained fight, then keep working slowly for as long as you can. Look for natural rhythms and moments when you can get good eye contact, then work them into the action and become familiar with them.

Actors need to know the fight much better than they need to know their lines. Let's face it, if an actor says the wrong line – or forgets their line – it is unlikely to result in physical injury and a visit to hospital.

Once both actors are consistently demonstrating a control over the techniques, good safe distance, and correct stage positioning, then they can be encouraged to start finding their way towards performance pace. Push the energy and intention levels a little further each time you run the sequence. But feel free to come back to the slow rehearsal at any time to check and correct any issues that you notice. Remember, you should be aiming to reach performance pace in time for the dress rehearsal or the technical rehearsal.

## Summary

- Keep it simple.

- Choose moves appropriate for the character and situation.

- Work out your distances and moments of eye contact.

- Allow the fight to build to a climax.

- Allow plenty of rehearsal time.

- Make sure you record it somehow. Write it down and film it if possible.

- Performance pace is your goal, not your starting point.

FIGHTING

The aim of this chapter has been to give you an understanding of how to stage and rehearse a short fight or a brief moment of violence on stage – safely. Hopefully it will help those of you in amateur theatres, universities, schools and fringe productions to maintain a level of safety and dramatic effectiveness in what you do. You should now have knowledge of how to create a simple fight sequence, how to record it, how and when to rehearse that sequence.

And hopefully it will help you understand when you need to call on the services of a fight director.

Above all else, *be safe*. Only then can you really begin to have fun!

# Further Information

The aim of this book is to give as many people as possible access to basic information that will keep them safe when performing violence on stage. If it prevents one person from getting hurt then it has been a success.

I hope it has also inspired you to learn more and train in class with a qualified teacher. I teach regular classes on Monday nights for anyone who wants to learn at the Birmingham School of Acting (www.bcu.ac.uk/acting). We cover Unarmed Combat during the first term, Rapier & Dagger in the second term, and a different weapon in the third term. You can enrol for the whole year or for any single term. I also teach regular courses at City Lit (www.citylit.ac.uk) in central London.

Details of all the courses I teach can be found at: www.stagecombatuk.com

The British Academy of Stage & Screen Combat (BASSC) is the UK's leading provider of stage combat training. They run regular courses throughout the year in London, Manchester and Stratford-upon-Avon. BASSC teachers also run courses in Glasgow, Norwich, Bath, Bournemouth and elsewhere. Details of all courses can be found on their website: www.bassc.org

You can also find the BASSC and Stage Combat UK on Facebook and Twitter.

# Acknowledgements

My eternal thanks to Matt Applewhite at Nick Hern Books, who first approached me about two years ago and asked the innocuous question, 'Have you ever thought about writing a book?' Thanks, too, to my editor, Benet Catty; to Jodi Gray for designing such a refreshingly clear book on this subject; and to Tim Digby-Bell for developing the accompanying website.

Thanks to my fellow teachers and members of the British Academy of Stage & Screen Combat. They have been my friends, my family, my professional support – as well as my teachers and my students. The passion and dedication they show to this art truly humbles me, and I am immensely grateful to them.

Many thanks to my wonderful photographic models and assistants – Enric Ortuño and Yarit Dor – who gave up their time and their skill to help me put the photos and videos together. And to Rob Leonard, my uncompromising photographer, without whose skill this book would look much poorer.

But I reserve my especial thanks for Richard Ryan, who has been my teacher, my guide and my mentor throughout my entire career. Thank you for taking the time to talk to me on the phone all those years ago, for all your encouragement along the way – and for your friendship.

*R.B.*

# Index of Techniques and Videos

INDEX

Watch the videos at
**www.stagecombatbook.com**

**www.stagecombatbook.com**
**www.nickhernbooks.co.uk**

facebook.com/nickhernbooks

twitter.com/nickhernbooks